Cats

Our Affectionate Friends

Cats
Our Affectionate Friends

All possible care has been taken in the making of this book. Nonetheless, no liability can be assumed for the information contained in it. Neither the author nor the translator nor the publisher can be held responsible for damages resulting from information in this book that is not in accordance with the current legal regulations in Great Britain, or from damages that result from the practical information in the book.

© Honos Verlag GmbH, a subsidiary of
VEMAG Verlags- und Medien Aktiengesellschaft, Cologne
www.apollo-intermedia.de

Author: Antje Breuer
Complete production: Honos Verlag GmbH, Cologne
Printed in Poland

Table of Contents

Introduction

"God invented the cat so that man would have a tiger to caress in his home." Victor Hugo

The cat is a being that cannot be compared with any other house pet. Despite domestication the cat remains today what it always was: a velvet-pawed individualist with sharp claws, who is gentle and affectionate but also proud and continually protecting its independence. So it's no coincidence that there are no cat lovers among the dictators in history.

Anyone who wants to live harmoniously under one roof with a cat must be tolerant and respect the wishes of their four-legged partner. Kitties do not let themselves be owned by people: they associate with humans when they have a desire for human affection. Cats offer the same consideration that they expect for their own emotions, and they return any affection they receive with interest.

It is a requirement, however, that one make the effort to understand cat language, which is by no means limited to the meow. Kitties, which are both much loved and much hated, are neither deceitful nor cunning. Anyone who correctly interprets the distinctive body language with which the velvet-pawed individualist expresses desires and fears will never feel the claws that cat haters dread. Since no other house pet radiates so much peace, satisfaction and harmony, cats are ideal partners for both younger and older single people, as well as for families with children. It has long since been proven that the "domestic tiger's" velvet paws and purring serve as an excellent therapy for dealing with dark thoughts, anxiety, loneliness and stress.

Cats are not only exemplary in their cleanliness, they also adapt well to all sorts of places and do not demand much of their surroundings. In comparison to other house pets they are particularly easy to care for and do not resent occasionally being left alone. This very trait sadly often leads people to decide all too lightly to bring darling little feline bundles into their lives—only to give them up just as quickly.

Millions of cats end up in animal shelters annually in the UK, and countless more are simply left to their own devices in the streets, especially during holiday time. A sudden separation from people leaves its traces in the sensitive feline soul, often with irreparable consequences. Whether house cat or pedigree cat, the feline values its human companion more than any other of its own kind.

Anyone who wants to adopt a cat must be aware of what responsibility that decision entails and be prepared to accept the cat as it is, with all the qualities of its individual character — for its entire life. Because cats can live as long as 20 years, in adopting a cat, one is accepting a responsibility for a lengthy period of time. This responsibility includes having your cat sterilised, having your male neutered or your female spayed to prevent the births of yet more animals who will later have no home. More than any other animal, the four-legged feline housemate requires human affection. And cats need human affection not just as young kittens, but as fully grown cats, as well.

The Cat:
A Friend to Humanity

The powerful and very timid European Wildcat was long regarded as the original ancestor of our house cat.

Today we believe that our house cats are descended from the smaller and more slender African or Nubian Wildcat.

Opposite page: Wildcat

How Cats Became Friends with People

The cat is a puzzling creature with a history full of secrets. A whole series of legends exists regarding the origins of the cat, some of which go back as far as the seventh millennium B.C.E. After cen-

turies of research, we are fairly certain today that our cats are descended from the African or Nubian Wildcat (*Felis silvestris lybica*). The African Wildcat is small and slender with a narrow head, large ears, a large, pointed tail and a short, sand-coloured to reddish brown spotted or striped coat. The European Wildcat (*Felis silvestris silvestris*), which for a long time was thought to be the original ancestor of our modern domestic cat, is by contrast very timid, has a compact physique, a wide head and a short, thick tail.

Scholars are not of one mind even today about where and when the cat first became a house pet: was it as early as 7000 years B.C.E. in Jericho or was it in the sixth millennium B.C.E. in Anatolian Hacilar? Finds of statuettes of women playing with cats are offered as evidence for the second theory. The oldest unambiguous evidence for cats as house pets is about 5000 years old and comes from Egypt. Mouse predators came to where people stored their grain and protected the supplies from the nibbling rodents. The ancient Egyptians thanked

the cats for this labour with love, honour and care. Cats were considered holy and inviolable.

The cat became a godly being, cared for by highly regarded cat priests and cat high priests, who did not move from the side of a temple cat. The temple of the fertility goddess Bastet, who was represented with the body of a woman and the head of a cat, was a site of pilgrimage for cat worshippers. When a cat died, it was embalmed and ceremonially laid into sanctified graves at the temple cat cemetery in the city of Bubastis in eastern part of the Nile River delta. As a symbol of grief, owners shaved off their eyebrows.

The killing of a cat was severely punished, including in many cases with capital punishment. The veneration of the cat went so far that the Egyptians even lost a battle on the animal's account. After a long, fruitless attempt to conquer the Egyptian city of Pelusion, the Persian king Cambyses had his warriors tie a cat to his shoulders in 525 B.C.E. His wager paid off. The Egyptians gave up without any resistance.

Only much later did the house cat, presumably from Egypt, make it to India. Even today Moslems and Hindus regard cats as holy. Prophet Mohammed, the founder of Islam, was among the great lovers of cats in history and enacted stringent laws for the protection of cats.

In ancient China, too, cats were appreciated as more than just mouse and rat hunters. The Chinese word "Mao" means both "cat" and "eighty years old". The cat was considered a symbol of luck and of a long life. The Chinese also believed that like people, cats have souls.

In Japan magical powers were ascribed to cats. They acted as protectors of silkworm breeding and they guarded holy scriptures in temples from rats. The imperial family gave worthy ministers a cat as a gift. People who owned a cat were considered refined and wealthy.

Through legionnaires, merchants and monks, cats came to Greece and Italy, where the cat became a symbol of freedom and independence. A cat graced the coat-of-arms of the noble Neapolitan clan "della Gata", and a cat lay at the feet of the goddess of freedom in the Roman temple to Tiberius Gracchus.

The Romans brought the first house cats to England. There, too, they were prized as mouse hunters and were treated exceptionally well. They guarded the king's granaries, and in South Wales there was even a law enacted to protect house cats. In Ireland, cats were consid-

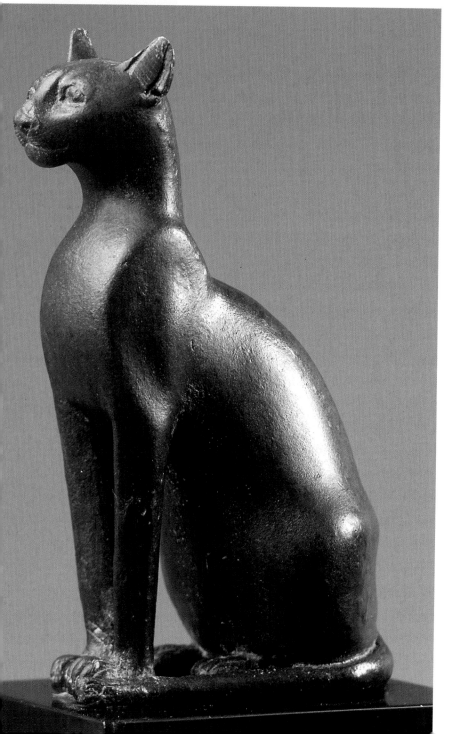

The bronze statue of an Egyptian temple cat that was worshipped as the holy animal of the goddess Bastet.

ered bringers of good luck and lucky spirits, and the leader of the Scottish clan Chattan was proud of the name "Great Cat". From England, the cat made its way into other European countries and accompanied the first European settlers into the New World, as well.

By the Middle Ages, however, the time of peaceful feline life was over for several centuries. Witch hunts meant persecution of cats and their owners. After having granted cats godly worship, cats—black ones in particular—were now said to embody evil. They were hunted, tortured in the most barbarous ways and killed.

Superstitious people today still believe that a black cat crossing one's path portends of bad luck. Many people also find cats mysterious and creepy: despite

their domestication, cats have preserved their individuality and their majestic gait. People who fear them don't see the velvet paws, but only the claws. They consider cats deceitful and cunning, they fear the cat's penetrating gaze and resent that cats, unlike dogs, do not subordinate themselves to people. It's revealing that almost all dictators in history have been cat haters. In the meantime, cats have overtaken dogs in ranking among house pets. In the UK alone, there are over nine million cats living in households with people. Is there any better evidence for the friendship between four-legged felines and people?

Velvet Paws Stroke the Soul

Cats give more than they take. They are gentle and affectionate, devoted and clean, and make no great demands of either their people or their surroundings. Cats can offer single people of any age the feeling that they are needed, and children learn mutual respect, tolerance and consideration from them. Their purr is music to the ears of any cat owner. Velvet paws stroke the soul.

"He makes himself the companion of your hours of solitude, melancholy and toil. He remains for whole evenings on

Black cats had a hard lot in the Middle Ages. During the time of witch hunts, they were hunted, cruelly tortured and killed. Superstitious people today still avoid black cats.

Information

Cats are distinct individualists who never do what people expect of them. Cats choose to attach themselves to people, and this is not the only respect in which cats are selective. It is exactly this quality, however, that cat admirers value.

In ancient Egypt, cats were embalmed and ceremonially buried. (Both statues pictured here can be seen in the Kestner Museum, Hanover.)

More and more men are discovering a love for cats.

Single people in particular, both young and older, enjoy cuddling with their kitties. Purring helps one forget loneliness and problems, and it makes us happier and more satisfied.

your knee, uttering his contented purr, happy to be with you." Many psychologists and doctors concur with nineteenth-century French writer Théophile Gautier that loneliness is well treated with a cat—more effectively and safely than with pills. This assertion is borne out by numerous studies which prove that cats radiate harmony and satisfaction and that they distract us from dark thoughts and worries.

Seven hundred cat owners took part in a broad study by the German psychologist Reinhold Bergler. The result: they are happier and more balanced than people without cats. "In people who continually live with cats, certain distinct emotional deficits, fears and anxieties, as well as feelings of loneliness and the psychologically and medically negative effects of such emotional states do not occur."

The American psychologist Eileen B. Karsh determined at the conclusion of a study of 17 solitary senior citizens averaging 59 years of age that a cat can positively influence one's life and state

of health. The seniors with cats felt less lonely, depressed or anxious. Four of the cat owners experienced a decrease in blood pressure and two who were diabetic had lower blood sugar levels.

The first experiments allowing residents of senior citizen homes to bring their cats with them are now running. These, too, confirm that these people are more psychologically balanced, more satisfied and healthier because they have a task and responsibility. When the cat owner dies, another resident takes over the care of the cat.

Studies of children and young adults also confirm the positive influence of cats on people's emotional state and behaviour: nervous people become more quiet, aggressive people become more peaceful, lonely people become happier. These studies underscore the opinion of veterinarian and animal welfare advocate Dr. Michael W. Fox that cats express their affection "in the gentlest possible way". Cats are friends and soulmates to people in all stages of life.

Cats and children can be a wonderful team, but both sides have to learn how to get along with the other first.

Children can learn a great deal from the four-legged individualists: cleanliness, tenderness and, most importantly, consideration for the wishes of another.

Cats are not Stuffed Animals

Cats are living beings who are born individualists and remain that way throughout their lives. People often forget this when they see cute little bundles of wool tumble around in play and conquer human hearts instantly with their velvet paws and gentle purring. Love at first sight, however, should not mislead anyone into adopting a cat without due consideration. A cat is not a stuffed animal that one can cuddle on demand and then simply set in a corner. The cat is the one who determines when and with whom she cuddles.

The partnership between a person and a cat functions only with consideration for each other's feelings and habits. Anyone who brings a cat into the house is assuming responsibility for an animal that reacts very sensitively and that despite domestication has retained its own nature. Responsibility is not limited to feeding and other physical care. Respect for the feline housemate, who can develop character traits as varied as any

15

cats before taking any definite decisions. One cannot predict whether an adorable kitten will later be a peaceful housemate or a claw-baring cat, whether it will be cuddly and affectionate or prefer to retire in solitude to a quiet corner. Just like human siblings, cats from a single litter can develop in very different ways.

And so it doesn't hurt to consider carefully and ahead of time what various possible faults a cat might have and to weigh precisely whether one is ready to accept the risk of these possible liabilities of cat ownership. This is especially true for cats who would be living with a family. The desire for the cat must not come from just one member of the family: the entire household must welcome a cat. Those who have the least bit of doubt should make do with a stuffed animal instead of a cat to spare themselves and the cat disappointments.

It should also be said that no animal, and in particular a cat, should ever be a surprise gift, no matter how well meaning. No matter how great the joy of the first moment, both giver and receiver are rarely aware of the consequences. A cat is not an object one can dispose of at will. If a cat is on someone's wish list,

Even as kittens, cats already know exactly what they want. Adopting a cat means not only assuming responsibility for its feeding and physical care, it also means maintaining respect and consideration for the individual character of this sensitive animal.

Looking at playful little kittens, one can forget all too easily that they have not only velvet paws but claws as well. In no time at all a cute little bundle of wool will turn into a full-grown house tiger, who was born an individualist and will remain so for the rest of its life.

person, is equally as important as feeding and physical care.

Cats are easy to care for. They are clean and quiet and they don't have to be taken outside three times a day. If these are someone's main arguments for acquiring a cat, however, the relationship between that someone and their cat will end in a fiasco sooner or later. Animal welfare advocates can attest to the shockingly high number of cats that end up on the streets and in animal shelters every year. Anyone who is considering adopting a cat should be well informed about the character and peculiarities of

Even when cats come across as independent and unproblematic, the new owner must plan sufficient time for feeding, physical care and cuddling the new cat.

give them a certificate for a cat and then afterwards consider together whether and when to redeem it.

In addition, if you rent your home, make certain ahead of time that cat ownership is allowed in your home: take a glance through your rental contract or speak directly with the landlord. Try to ascer-tain ahead of time, too, whether you might not have an allergic reaction to cat hairs. Pet the cats of your neighbours, friends or acquaintances. If no allergic reactions seem to emerge and all the other conditions and requirements are fulfilled, you may in good conscience join the great circle of cat lovers.

One cannot tell by looking at young kittens how they will later develop. Even siblings from the same litter can later develop entirely different characters and habits—they can be very affectionate or they could also be very brusque.

The adoption of a cat means accepting a responsibility, including for the time when the animal is no longer a cute little baby.

One of the universally beloved cat places is the windowsill.

The Cat Person

"Til death do us part" applies not just to newlyweds, but to the partnership between a person and a cat as well. After all, cats can live for 20 years and longer, accompanying people for a considerable period of time. And along with their people, cats get older, too. This is another reason to consider very thoughtfully what you want from a cat: do you love only darling little kittens or are you a true cat person?

All the joy and tenderness that a cat brings into a person's life aside, one must not forget that a cat requires a certain amount of investment, even if one receives a kitten as a gift. More than just the money required for food, physical care and immunisations, cats require generous amounts of your time if they are to grow up healthy and content—time for playing and time for mutual, loving affection. One of the great virtues that characterises a cat person is tolerance. Because a cat does not allow itself to be drilled and trained like a dog, one must be entirely willing to toss out any number of rigid principles if one does not wish to make a cat's life unnecessarily difficult. One such widespread "principle", for example, is that bedrooms should be taboo for cats. But cats will not restrict their activities to conform to arbitrary human notions. They don't allow someone else to decide where and when to sleep, and they'll find their own cosy spots, preferably on a pillow, at the foot of a bed or in a person's favourite chair. This problem usually solves itself with the cat as victor, because no one manages to scare the cat away. And even scaring a cat away wouldn't prevent a determined animal from jumping back up the very next moment onto the favoured spot to curl up and relax.

"Principle" number two: the cat must never be on the table and must eat only from the cat bowl in its proper place. Ah, but precisely because of its height, the table offers a better view than the couch. And when the family is sitting together all cosy at the coffee table, a true cat friend will look away when kitty laps up a bit of delicious cream.

strewn about or get stuck in the cat's paws, only to be traipsed across the entire house.

This, too, is something to consider: cats may occasionally vomit on a valuable carpet or the couch if they have eaten too quickly or to dislodge a hairball or cat grass. If this would lead to a raving fit, you should probably forgo having a pet. You may also have to give up a houseplant or two, both because some plants are dangerous to animals and because a plant may die if the cat takes a liking to nibbling on it.

Just like people, loneliness makes cats ill, too. Before adopting a cat, it's very important to consider who will care for

All cats will search for their favourite place in the house or garden, and unfortunately, that is often your favourite place, too.

Purebred cats such as this Russian Blue also have claws. The finest scratching post and cat climbing tree around is no guarantee, with indoor cats in particular, that couches and chairs will forever be spared the traces of cat scratches.

Where there are cats, there are cat hairs, unless one decides to adopt the entirely hairless Sphynx, which is bred in the U.S.A. Any cat owner who doesn't want to be a slave to the household will decide to simply live with cat hairs. Even the loveliest little basket with the softest cushion will not stop a cat from trying out all the spots on the couch. And it's almost always futile to try to protect the couch by laying a blanket on it: a cat will in all probability lie down exactly beside the blanket or seek out a new spot.

Cats have claws, and they don't always use the scratching post to sharpen them, either. With indoor cats, in particular, it's all but certain that they will not miss the opportunity to leave their mark on couch and chair. One must also become accustomed to having the cords from curtains and clothing pulled when the cat starts hunting flies or when it's been dozing comfortably in someone's lap and then stretches. And once in a while, when a bit of playing goes too far for the cat, human skin might get a scratch. Here and there an object or two might also get broken in the process.

Especially with indoor cats, the litter tray can become quite an annoyance. At least cats are clean animals who carefully bury their business. It doesn't always suffice to keep it clean and freshly changed. A grain or two of litter will inevitably be

One Cat or Two?

There are many factors that speak in favour of adopting not just one but two cats at the same time. Behavioural researchers believe that cats in pairs are happier. The cat owner also has double the pleasure when observing the cats play together and clean each other.

The second cat cannot, however, serve as a replacement for human attention. Professor and animal behavior researcher Paul Leyhausen determined in his decades of studying cats that the relationships between each individual cat and a person are much closer than those between the two cats ever become. The practical implication of this is that one must divide one's affection and attention evenly between both cats. And cats have double the fun in playing with each other if their human also participates.

If one knows in advance that one will be out of the house for much of the time, it is certainly a good idea to adopt two

A desk isn't just a place for working, it's a place to make yourself comfortable.

Many houseplants are dangerous to cats.

the animal during short trips or holidays and if you are ill. These are all precautions that a genuine cat person simply takes for granted. And finally, one thing should be clear to anyone who invites a cat into their home. It is not the person who keeps the cat; it is the cat who keeps the person.

cats. It's true that cats spend a great deal of their day sleeping, dozing and grooming, but if they are left alone too much of the time they often become aggressive. With a four-legged playmate

they cope better with the absence of their human companion.

It's ideal to adopt two cats at once—one male and one female is best—from the same litter. Two from the same litter already know each other, and they are playmates from the very first moment. It is also possible to introduce a second cat into the household later. If one follows a few basic rules, the two cats will quickly adjust to one another and become friends.

To rule out potential power battles, the second cat should be younger than the cat already in the home, and the newling should be as young as possible. The younger cat will adapt without difficulty and accept the seniority of the older cat. If the older cat is female, she will initially

A pair of cats requires time to become a well-adjusted team. Competitive battles can be overcome quickly, however, with a few simple tricks.

Cats seek out their own favourite places.

21

When kittens of one litter grow up together, they become inseparable friends. They sleep curled up next to each other and even clean each other.

have its own food and water dishes, as well as its own litter tray. It's best not to bring the second cat into the house oneself, but have someone else bring it in for you. And even though it's an adorable little bundle of fur, ignore it for a time and give the older animal especially demonstrative affection. This way no jealousy will develop. The two animals will quickly sort things out amongst themselves. And if they occasionally have little tussles and scuffs, people should not interfere. As is so often the case with children, the cats will usually sort out their differences quickly and a short time later will be the best of friends again, lying cuddled up close to each other.

Cats don't feel lonely when they are alone, but if their person cannot spend lots of time with them, they often enjoy four-legged playmates.

protest the intruder's presence with hissing and a bottle-brush tail, but she will quickly develop maternal instincts and make the kitten's adjustment easier.

In order to prevent struggles for dominance from the outset, each cat should

How and Where to Find Your Cat

Which Cat Should I Choose?

*Cats observe their sur-
roundings with curiosity.*

Once one has carefully considered all the advantages and disadvantages of adopting a cat and the desire for a cat is as strong as ever, the next question is what kind of cat to adopt. This is by no means merely a matter of whether one should choose a completely ordinary cat or one with noble lineage. In both cases one ought to consider what sort of environment the cat will be living in and what sort of character traits one expects of one's feline housemate. This will spare both you and the animal later disappointments.

Problems will inevitably arise, for example, if you live in an apartment in the city with a small balcony and you adopt

*Indoor cats live longer.
If they've never known
the freedom of roaming
outside the house, they're
content to enjoy the view
from the windowsill.*

a cat that spent the early weeks of its life out in the open in nature and has had its first little successes as a hunter. Anyone living in a city apartment should choose a cat that was born and has spent its early life indoors.

There are many conflicting opinions regarding whether cats should be indoor or outdoor creatures. While some believe that only outdoor cats are genuinely content, those who defend indoor cats point out the many dangers that threaten a cat out of doors. One thing is certain: indoor cats live significantly longer than outdoor cats. It is a fact that thousands cats are run over by cars annually—this is the most common cause of cat death in the UK—and that thousands more are shot. An indoor cat not only lives longer, it is also entirely content to be indoors as long as it knows no other environment and as long as the people in the household spend sufficient time playing and exchanging affection with the cat. If a garden is to be part of the cat's future territory, it won't hurt if the cat learned mouse hunting from its mother. Cat owners should take a few precautions, however, to protect their pets from the threats of cars, hunters and poison.

Another important consideration is the cat's temperament, and in this respect cats are as varied as people. It is as difficult to predict the temperament of a kitten when it becomes a full-grown cat

as it is in human children. One can make a basic generalisation, however, that shorthaired cats are likely to have more lively temperaments than longhaired cats, and that animals with lighter coats react more sensitively than cats with dark coats. This guideline is valid for both ordinary cats and pedigree cats, but it is no guarantee. There are exceptions that prove the rule, but anyone who would prefer a calmer feline housemate will certainly enjoy a gentle, timid Persian cat more than a lively and talkative Siamese.

Pedigree cats will subject a person to the fewest surprises regarding both character and external characteristics, such as the adult size, colour and coat markings. On the other hand, naturally, the surprise effect itself can be particularly delightful.

A decision for an ordinary or a pedigree cat is, of course, a question of price as well. Cute little kittens without any documented lineage can be adopted for little or no money, whereas one has to spend three to five hundred pounds or more for a pedigree cat. And pedigree cats are as a rule more sensitive and delicate than ordinary house cats.

Regardless of the cat's lineage, if there will be other animals or children in the household it's best to choose a kitten that has encountered that kind of companionship in its previous environment. This way, the cat won't startle and bolt with every loud noise or extend its claws at every clumsy attempt at petting on the part of a child, and it makes settling in and getting used to each other that much easier.

Outdoor cats enjoy strolling around out in the open. Many dangers threaten them out of doors, however, from which cat owners must protect them as much as possible.

Female Cat or a Tom?

Toms are said to be more devoted and sociable than female cats, but this can easily be the other way around. If having kittens is not a concern, it's not important whether one chooses a female or a male cat.

If you do not wish to make your own life, as well as that of your cat, into a living hell you will have your little tiger neutered as soon as it is sexually mature. Thanks to advances in veterinary sciences, this procedure is as easy for females as it is for males. In contrast to sterilisation, in which the spermatic cord in the male and the fallopian tubes in the female are just cut, in neutering or spaying the sexual organs—the testicles or the ovaries—are removed entirely under full anaesthesia. Castrated male cats are calmer and more trusting, they wander less, and most importantly the "spraying" with which they mark their territory is diminished. Spayed female cats don't go into heat.

It is not without reason that cats have long been a symbol of fertility. They become sexually mature at just eight or ten months of age, and a female can produce litters of five to six kittens two to three times annually. After a decade,

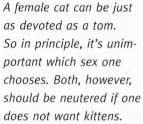

A female cat can be just as devoted as a tom. So in principle, it's unimportant which sex one chooses. Both, however, should be neutered if one does not want kittens.

the children of a female cat can accrue to over 80 million animals! The result is that many young kittens are put to sleep or simply abandoned because no one takes them in.

If a female cat's fallopian tubes are severed she will not produce young, but she will go into heat several times a year. During these periods she will eat little, roll around and emit sometimes deafeningly loud cries. The cat and her owner can be spared this nerve-wracking cycle by having the cat spayed.

Male cats who live indoors must be neutered: no one can stand the odour of their territorial markings. People who allow unneutered male cats to roam freely outdoors are not just irritating the neighbours, they are playing with their cats' lives. When an unneutered tom wanders about in search of love, he can't be restrained and is blind to danger. It is often a question of time before he ends up under a car. Neutering and spaying is therefore the best protection for cats. They are a must if one adopts a male-female pair from a single litter.

While it used to be argued that it was best to spay a female cat only after she produced her first litter, today we are advised to neuter and spay cats early. Although many people still believe that the animal is psychologically and physically altered by the procedure, this idea has been disproved. Physical differences are evident only in male cats that are neutered too young: they may become heavy and lethargic. If the procedure is done just after the start of sexual maturity, nothing in a cat's figure or behaviour will be changed. After a few days the procedure will be entirely forgotten, and cats are generally even more devoted and frisky than ever.

Which Season Produces the Healthiest Kittens

In our latitude, the sexual life of cats takes place primarily between February

and July. The kittens are born almost exactly 63 days after copulation, most of them in early May. The old-fashioned notion that "May kittens" are healthier and more robust than kittens born in August is accurate today only for mother cats who have given birth and raised their kittens without any human care. There is no reason to insist on a "May kitten".

If a new kitten won't have the opportunity to play in a garden, it is actually

A female cat can bear young two to three times annually.

training them in cat cleanliness. After about four weeks, kittens are weaned from their mother's milk, get their first solid food and make their first tentative explorations.

This is also the time when the kittens make their first acquaintance with mice, at first supplied by their mother. And thus they gradually become hunters themselves. The urge to hunt does not fade in an indoor cat. Stalking, ambushing and catching prey are the favourite games of all young kittens, and it remains so in grown cats, too.

So that the kittens stay healthy, they should receive their first vaccine against feline enteritis and feline 'flu at eight to nine weeks. Booster shots are given four weeks later. In the meantime, the mother cat will have taught her children all the essential knowledge necessary for a cat's life. She distances herself from her kittens, who at ten to twelve weeks —if they're lucky—find a new and loving home with a "cat person".

The Right Way to Find a Cat

If you are hoping to find a completely normal little kitty to be your feline housemate, it's best to listen around among family and friends to find out

When a cat mother bears her young under the auspices of human care, kittens born in August are as healthy and lively as "May kittens". They learn everything a cat needs to know from their mother.

Inquire at your veterinarian or at a cat or animal protection league whether they know of a litter of kittens seeking new homes.

advisable to wait for an August kitten. The chances are greater then that it won't have much experience out in the wild and that it will be a content indoor cat that doesn't miss being outdoors.

Kittens are born blind and open their eyes only after seven to eight days, and they can only see and hear properly after about four weeks. Their senses of smell and touch are well developed from early on, since those senses help them find their way to their mother's milk. Cat babies spend their first few weeks nursing and sleeping, all cuddled up close together.

The female cat is an exemplary mother who takes care of her kittens from the very first moment, tending to them and

whether there are kittens waiting to be born somewhere nearby. A good place to start is at the veterinarian's office. Since veterinarians know mother cats and since they immunise kittens, they will often be able to recommend some addresses, or there will even be announcements hanging in the veterinarian's office.

Or look into the daily newspaper. There are always announcements in the classified advertisements, many or few depending on the time of year, for toilet-trained cats needing homes. In many places there are also cat associations that are grateful to find takers for young kittens. If you cannot find these associations in your local telephone book, inquire at the Cats Protection charity (www.cats.org.uk) or at the Feline Advisory Board (www.fabcats.org) or at your local animal protection league. Another

option is to find the nearest animal shelter. Any number of healthy, immunised and neutered/spayed cats are waiting there for good homes.

Anyone who decides to adopt a pedigree cat is advised to buy the cat directly

Only after ten to twelve weeks does the mother cat begin to distance herself from her offspring. Kittens require this length of time to learn what they need to know for life.

A pedigree cat such as this Persian should be adopted only directly from a reputable breeder.

31

Cats who are raised in such enclosures often demonstrate psychological and even physical deficits later.

Animal shelters are full of cats young and old that are waiting for a new home.

from the breeder. But take care! As in other areas, there are disreputable people more concerned with money than the fate of the cats. One can obtain the addresses of reputable breeders from the various cat-breed associations and clubs. If one is not yet set on a particular breed, it is worthwhile to visit the cat exhibits that take place in various cities and times. There one can observe all the different long- and shorthaired breeds, make direct contact with breeders and learn about the signature traits and characteristics of the various breeds.

Reputable breeders are those who never sell a cat "blind". They gather precise information about the environment in which the kitten will be living. This is true, by the way, not only of pedigree cats. Animal shelters and people posting ads who are concerned about the future life of their precious young charges will carefully screen anyone interested in one of their cats. To be very certain, some breeders don't allow the animal to be picked up, but bring the kitten to its new home personally. Under no circumstances should one purchase a cat, ordinary or purebred, from an animal dealer. These animals are often raised in kitten mills and separated from their mothers far too early. In the sensitive soul of the cat, that almost always leads to psychological and even physical damage that

become evident only long after the purchase has been made. Many of these cats finally end up in animal shelters, because their new owners are disappointed and overwhelmed by them.

The Protection of Cats

Many cats are given up to animal shelters annually, the majority during holiday time. The Cats Protection League, established in 1927, tells a story of endless misery, of cats that are abandoned and wander about aimlessly without a place to call home. The attempts of the members and volunteers of this organisation to feed these hungry animals, as well as to capture and neuter them, are but a drop in the bucket.

Considering how overpopulated animal shelters are, the Cats Protection League considers it irresponsible to allow cats which are not specifically required for breeding to reproduce in this day and age. A single female cat may have as many as 20,000 descendants in only five years. Cats Protection appeals to all cat owners to neuter or spay their pets at the onset of sexual maturity.

Many cat and animal protection societies, as well as most veterinarians, are very critical of breeding cats whose signature traits are caused by birth defects. Manx cats, which have no tail, are among these. Without a tail, they are missing an essential tool for balance in jumping and climbing. They have a hobbled gait and frequently suffer from muscle and nerve damage. Rex cats, with their sparse, crimped coat of fur, also have short, thin whiskers that significantly restrict their ability to feel. And the completely hairless Sphynx cats are viable only in certain conditions. Animal protection advocates consider this kind of breeding a form of torture and urge a fundamental prohibition against breeding with defective genes as well as a prohibition of "hobby breeding" through a house pet breeding law.

Breeders of white cats came into the line of fire in Germany in 1994, since the offspring of white cats, and blue-eyed white cats in particular, are likely to be

Sphynx cats, which are entirely hairless, can only live under certain circumstances.

Cats are simply abandoned by owners with no conscience, especially during holiday time, and they roam around hungrily.

White cats with blue eyes are usually deaf.

law reads in part: "It shall be prohibited to breed vertebrates or to change them through procedures of biotechnology or genetic engineering if it must be expected that the offspring, the animals altered by biotechnology or genetic engineering or their offspring due to hereditary factors are lacking parts of the body or organs for species-specific use or they are unfit or deformed thereby causing pain, suffering or harm."

Another problem are the many cats that are allowed to go outside and never return from their wanderings. All too often they end up in the hands of unscrupulous animal catchers and from there go to dealers or laboratories as experimental subjects. To make it harder for such people to do this, the RSPCA and other animal protection organisations recommend microchip implantion (done by any veterinarian) and registration of all cats. This increases the chance that a missing pet can be reunited with its owner.

deaf. One court, calling on paragraph 11b of the German Animal Protection Act, which expressly forbids breeding of abnormalities that cause suffering, found the breeder of white Persian cats guilty and fined her 250 Euros. The text of the

Older people in particular enjoy the affection and love of a velvet-pawed housemate. Because a cat can live for as long as 20 years, though, people of advanced age should consider adopting an older cat.

A nominal fee for young kittens reduces the risk that they will be abandoned all over again or that they will end up in a laboratory as experimental subjects or in the hands of dealers with no conscience.

Healthy young kittens have a glossy coat.

The love and care of the mother cat in the first few weeks of kittens' lives is irreplaceable.

Another aspect of looking out for a cat's best interests is to consider its lifespan. Because cats can live as long as 20 years, prospective cat owners who are advanced in years might consider adopting a cat with a life expectancy similar to their own. This may spare the cat the sad fate of wasting away in a shelter without the comfort of their beloved person. Despite the earnest promises of relatives and friends, it may well be that no one is prepared to take on responsibility for the cat after its owner passes away, and the cat itself may have to be put to sleep.

Others who want to be certain that their beloved cat will be well cared for can turn to the National Animal Welfare Trust, which offers assistance to elderly pet owners in case of sudden illness or other incapacity. NAWT also helps find homes for animals who have lost their owners, and it is the organisation's policy never to put a healthy animal to sleep. The Cats Protection also has a network of cat rescue shelters throughout the UK. The websites for these organisations, which are listed on page 189, contain more specific information.

In the interest of animal protection the Cats Protection League urges that kittens never be given away for free, but that there always be a nominal fee for them. This reduces the danger that the animal will not be adopted impulsively and then treated badly, under the motto that what costs nothing is worth nothing. This also reduces the chances that a cat will end up in the hands of unscrupulous animal dealers or as the subject of laboratory experiments. Anyone who is truly interested in cats as living beings will not shy away from a small expense to compensate for the costs of feeding, care and vaccinations.

Don't Buy a "Cat in the Sack"

"Trust is good, control is better." This time-tested principle is something one

should embrace in the search for a kitten. Purchasing a cat is not a business to be conducted with one foot out the door. People who love their cats, who have

People who want to spare the animal and themselves from later disappointments will not buy a "cat in the sack".

Beauties such as these Balinese cats often need special care.

nothing to hide, who see in the mother cat's litter more than just another source of cash will themselves suggest to anyone who's interested that they take time to inspect the cats' living quarters, get to know the mother cat and observe the kittens at play.

If the kittens are far away from the vicinity of any human activity, isolated deep in the cellar or in a cage, leave immediately. If they live in the home, however, and the house doesn't reek of cat odours and the food dishes and litter trays seem to be clean, the first hurdle is overcome. Then take some time to observe the kittens as they tumble and play. Healthy young cats are cheerful and curious, they have a shiny coat, clear eyes and a clean nose. Their ears should also be clean and they shouldn't smell. Frequent head shaking indicates the presence of ear mites.

Perform a hearing test for white cats, in particular, by talking to them in a normal voice—without moving at all. If the cat does not react, it is presumably deaf, which occurs frequently in white cats. And carefully look into the cat's mouth. If it doesn't yet have all its teeth, it is still too young to be separated from its mother.

If all the kittens make a healthy first impression, then you have the burden of decision upon you. All the little fluff balls are cute, after all. One of the kittens may make the decision for you by not leaving your side and courting your love with purrs. This is how we acquired our cat Crumb, who was by no means the prettiest, the strongest or the liveliest of the litter, but who is as frisky today as a twelve-year-old black panther and is an exceptionally affectionate cat.

It speaks in favour of cat owners if they don't try to suggest which kitten one should choose but instead insist that you choose yourself. A responsible owner will present you with the immunisation certificate, let you know about feeding habits and possibly even ask you to sign a document stating that you will care for the kitten properly.

There are additional important factors to consider when purchasing a pedigreed cat. To be certain, one should purchase only a kitten with a recognised pedigree. Inquire, too, how many litters the mother cat has had in one year. Reputable organisations generally recognise and register only two litters per queen annually.

Depending on your own feelings and preferences, you can decide whether you have any ambition to show the cat at an exhibition or to breed. If so, you should learn ahead of time about the ideal type for that particular breed. Breeders differentiate between enthusiast animals, exhibition animals and breeding animals.

Young kittens shouldn't be separated from their mother too soon.

Their prices vary accordingly. A breeding animal is not allowed to have a single flaw in appearance and must correspond to the standard in every way.

In the interest of both parties, these criteria should be recorded in the purchase contract, which forms an important basis for any later disagreements. For the protection of the animal, many contracts contain a clause stating that the cat may not be given up or sold to a third person without the permission of the breeder. They reserve this explicit first right of purchase to spare the animal any possibly problematic change of ownership.

The purchase contract must contain all relevant data about the animal. The purchase price should include the pedigree and the immunisation certificate with proof of vaccination against feline 'flu and feline enteritis. Many breeders even have their cats immunised against feline leukaemia or at least have a feline leukaemia test done on their kittens before they sell them.

Young kittens are not wares to be purchased and sold blindly. Reputable cat owners will want to be assured that their kittens are going to the home of an animal friend who will give them plenty of affection.

Portraits of the Cat Breeds

An ordinary cat is for lay people indistinguishable from a pedigree cat: the differences lie in the colouring, the length of the fur and markings on the coat.

Breeding, Standards and Exhibitions

With or without a pedigree, a cat remains a cat. The ordinary house cat has a breed, too. And in terms of beauty, she can hold her own against the refined cats. The have the same gracious gait, the same basic characteristics, the same ways of relating and the same needs. Where they differ are simply in colour, length of fur and markings on the coat. The number of pedigree cat enthusiasts is on the rise, but 94% of all kitties are still completely ordinary house cats.

England is the cradle of cat breeding. The first organised cat exhibition took place in 1871 in the London Crystal Palace, and today there are around 50 recognised cat breeds. The traits specific to the breeds are described in great detail in standards established by umbrella organisations, including Fédération Inter-

nationale Féline (F.I.Fe), the Governing Council of the Cat Fancy (GCCF) and the Cat Fanciers' Association (CFA).

The National Cat Club (NCC), founded in 1887 by Mr Harrison Weir, sponsored that first cat show in 1871 and still sponsors the National Cat Show. The NCC's motto is "Beauty lives by Kindness".

In 1910, the Governing Council of the Cat Fancy (GCCF) was founded as the governing body of Cat Fancy in the United Kingdom, the feline equivalent of the Kennel Club. The GCCF registers pedigree cats in the UK, licenses judges and cat shows and advocates for pedigree cats. Many local and breed-specific clubs in the UK are members of the GCCF, and it registers about 32,000 pedigree cats annually. The GCCF sponsors the Supreme Cat Show.

The club Felis Britannica has provisional membership as the UK representative in FIFe after the Cat Association of Britain went into voluntary liquidation.

At cat shows sponsored by various associations and clubs, the cats are measured by judges against official standards set by FIFE, GCCF and/or CFA. Only cats who fulfil all the criteria and correspond to the ideal image will receive placements and awards.

Visitors to a cat exhibition are thus privileged to see the most beautiful representatives of the species. To exhibit, one is usually required to be a member of the federation or club, but one does not necessary have to have a cat with a noble pedigree. Ordinary domestic house cats can participate in the beauty contests, too. They are judged in a special class, in which beauty and quality of the coat are the top criteria.

Before the show, cats settle in and make themselves at home in their often lovingly furnished cages with exemplary patience. Veterinarians examine their hearts and kidneys as they arrive. Specially trained stewards later carry the cats, who almost never hiss or growl, to the judges, who know neither where they are from or to whom they belong. Every

A person who wants a pedigree cat such as this Russian Blue just to love can easily overlook small imperfections in appearance.

Even the Turkish Van doesn't have to comply with the standards 100% if breeding or exhibiting are not planned.

Information

People visiting a cat exhibition for the first time will initially be confused because they don't understand the jargon the breeders use (see the Glossary), they don't comprehend the judging system and because they don't know the relative rankings of the titles. Someone who would like to exhibit their own pedigreed cat for the first time stands before the same problem.

cat wears an assigned number on its cage, and anonymity is preserved until the end of the show.

The cats are divided into classes according to breed, colour, gender and previous exhibition results, and then the judges assess them according to the standards of their breed with an elaborate system of points. Different umbrella groups follow different award systems, so the titles awarded in GCCF shows differ from those awarded in CFA, both of which in turn differ from the FIFe system. It's all quite elaborate and complex, but to offer you an overview, the FIFe award system is described here.

The total number of points determines whether a cat receives a grade of Good,

One of the most well-known and popular pedigree cats is the Angora.

Carefully considered nutrition plays a major roll in breeding, too.

Very Good or Excellent. Excellent cats are deemed suitable for breeding without exception and may apply for the title of CAC (*Certificat d'Aptitude au Championat*), the Candidature for the Title of Champion. This is awarded when a cat has received the CAC at three exhibits.

In order to rise from Champion to International Champion, the cat must be awarded the title of CACIB (*Certificat d'Aptitude au Championat International de Beauté*) at three further exhibitions, and this must be judged by international judges. Participating in exhibitions abroad is generally required. Even as an international champion with the triple title of CAGCIB or CAGCI (*Certificat d'Aptitude au Grand Championat International de Beauté*), the cat has still not reached the top level of victory.

The next hurdle is the candidature for the title CACE (*Certificat d'Aptitude au Championat d'Europe*). The very highest award a cat can receive is the title CAGCE (*Certificat d'Aptitude au Grand Championat d'Europe*), which makes the cat the Grand Champion of Europe.

There is separate but similar judging for "altered" (neutered or spayed) cats. Altered cats cannot become Champions, however, but are called Premiers. Finally, there are further awards given in various categories such as Best of Variety, Best in Show and Supreme Beauty. International cat exhibitions are run according to the same basic scheme, with minor differences in the judging criteria and in the awarding of titles.

Cat exhibitions by reputable people are not buying shows, and this has its reasons. Despite required veterinary examinations and optimal hygiene, it is possible for an animal to become infected because of the great number of cats being shown. Reputable breeders first take their cats home, observe them closely and only then bring a cat to a person interested in it. This also limits spontaneous purchases, which all too often end up in suffering for the animal. If a breeder offers to sell an animal at an

A cat's character counts towards a judge's decision: in such a calm and proud pose these European Silver Tabbies have good chances at an exhibition.

This Havana Brown is posing with dignity for the judge's consideration.

exhibition, scepticism is called for. On the other hand, exhibitions are an ideal setting for breeders to mingle with each other and all kinds of people interested in cats. No other setting offers better opportunities for direct exchange of experience.

Cat Breeding is not a Business

No one will ever become wealthy through cat breeding. People who engage in serious and responsible cat breeding will get back in the price of purchase only what they have already spent in time and money for feeding, physical care, veterinary care, participation in exhibitions and travel costs. The price is determined by supply and demand, and prices fluctuate accordingly. Another matter to

Portraits of the Cat Breeds

be considered is that the number of kittens produced varies from breed to breed, and no litter consists exclusively of flawless kittens who will all later shine at exhibitions.

The standards established by the judges are quite variable from breed to breed. There is, however, a whole series of beauty flaws that are considered handicaps in all breeds and that mean "out" at any exhibit. To some degree, these flaws do not diminish the beauty of the cat at all in the eye of an ordinary cat lover. A person who just wants a cat to love can easily live with these beauty flaws. At exhibitions, however, these same beloved animals have no chance. These flaws, which have no affect on the cat's health or a person's ability to love the animal, include crossed eyes and a kink in the tail. Nor does an indentation in the brow area of the skull, a slightly lopsided jaw or a minor dental flaw have to have any relevance for the animal's health and well being.

A pronounced underbite or overbite in the jaw, a very narrow lower jaw or a crooked lower jaw can, however, become problematic at some point in time.

More serious failings are undersized nostrils or too pronounced a drop in the bridge of the nose. These can lead to difficulties in breathing, and too short a nose can also lead to blocked tear ducts. Deformations of the skeleton lead to dis-

qualification. If one observes a cat from the side, the chest should be symmetrically rounded and oval from the spinal column to the stern.

A serious flaw is dislocation of the knee cap, which is when the knee cap can slide from the front of the joint to the side. Cats with too many or too few claw find no mercy from the judges. An exhibition cat has four toes on each paw and a fifth toe on the hind side of each foreleg. A cat's condition, meaning the general impression it makes, plays an essential role in the judging: champions are clean and groomed, healthy, calm and cooperative.

An Abyssinian with her young.

These pretty Somali kittens might someday achieve victory at an exhibition. The critical eyes of the judges decide what constitutes flawless beauty in the particular breeds.

45

Longhaired Cats

Persians

Persian cats were already being bred in Asia centuries ago. They caused quite a sensation at the end of the nineteenth century at a cat exhibition in London, and today many people still consider them the epitome of feline beauty and a synonym for longhaired cats generally. They also continue to be one of the most well known and popular pedigree cats, and they offer the widest variation in colour. The variety of colours ranges from snow white to colourful to deep black.

Persian cats used to be called Angora cats because of their longhaired coats, named after the Turkish province of Angora (Ankara today). Only a few decades ago did the theory that Persian cats come from Persia and not from Turkey really gain acceptance. As early as 1521 the travelling scholar Pietro della Valle brought a Persian cat back to Italy from northern Iranian provinces.

After the Persian cats created a craze at the London Crystal Palace Exhibit and

Cream-coloured Persian cats: one of the many impressive colour variations of the breed today.

The first Persians were blue, white and black. The black coat develops only in fully grown cats.

47

Chinchilla Persians have glistening silve fur and green eyes surrounded by a dark rim.

A Red Persian with a distinct drop between the forehead and the nose.

Queen Victoria acquired a Blue Persian, these cats started from England on a victory lap around the whole world. While the first Persians were only black, white and blue, the standard today lists 85 colour variations.

White Persians have a special feature: their eyes are blue, orange or bicoloured, with one blue eye and the other copper-coloured or orange. The problem is that blue-eyed white Persians are almost always deaf. In addition to the single-

This black Smoke Persian is a cat of contrasts. Right: A cream-coloured Persian with a beautiful, almost pastel coat.

The markings on the coat of Tabby Persians must be distinct from one another, with a clear M on the brow.

coloured Persians without markings in white, black, blue, red, cream, chocolate and lilac, there are also Smoke Persians whose white or silver-white coats gradually fade into black, blue, chocolate, lilac or red toward the tip of the fur. This fading of one colour into another toward the tip of each hair is known as "tipping", and it appears on the back, head and paws, while the frill, flank and ear tufts are white.

The tipped Persians also include the Chinchilla, with a white undercoat and the coat on the back, flank, head, ears and tail tipped with black. An evenly distributed tipping lends the Chinchilla Persian a characteristic bright silver appearance. This cat's emerald or blue-green eyes are also very impressive.

Bicolour Persians are allowed to have as much as two-thirds of their coat coloured and as much as half white. Any spots in the face have to be evenly distributed and the eyes must be orange or copper-coloured. An especially pretty variation is the Tortoiseshell Persian, whose coat consists of large distinct and separate spots in black and red tones or in blue and cream combined with white.

Finally, there are Persian Tabbies. Their markings should be clearly discernable, with an M on the forehead. The throat and chest should be adorned with several complete rings, like necklaces, and "bracelets" around the legs.

One thing that all Persian cats have in common is their beautiful, thick, long,

There is are numerous variations of bicolour Persians.

Bicolour Persians are allowed to have as much as two-thirds of their coat colourful and only as much as half may be white.

Below and on the opposite page: Exotic Shorthairs have the same facial expression and physique as Persians, but they have a shorter coat that is much easier to care for.

silky coat with a decorative neck ruffle that covers the shoulders and spreads down the forelegs. This ruffle must be combed and brushed daily so that it remains beautiful and doesn't mat. The ruffle should fluff up away from the body and always move with the cat.

All Persians make a majestic impression with their compact round heads, their round eyes and their small, rounded ears, their short, broad noses with a distinctive kink at the bridge, their large to medium-large muscular bodies, their large round paws and their short, very bushy tails. Their character is equally majestic: they tend to be self-assured, calm, thoughtful and never obtrusive. The Persian is an ideal apartment cat, but this breed is not known to be an especially cuddly pet.

A matter that one should consider before adopting a Persian: these are not easy animals to care for. They are dependent on people for the care of their long, thick coats. An alternative is the shorthaired Persian, a breed called Exotic. This cat differs from its longhaired relative only in the length of its coat.

The Persian's extremely small nose with its noticeable kink is somewhat problematic, because although it lends this breed its distinctive sweet look, at the same time it represents a risk to the cat's health. The narrowing of the tear duct and nasal passages means that this cat can easily have difficulties breathing. And the large, round eyes are lovely, but they are also particularly sensitive.

Colourpoint

The Colourpoint, which was formerly called the Khmer Cat and is known in the USA as the Himalayan, resulted from a breeding of Siamese and Persian cats. The cat's origin has nothing to do with either the Cambodian people or with the Himalayas. The first Colourpoints were bred in the 1930s in the USA, and they were recognised in Europe in the mid-1950s. Most Colourpoints today, however, are still found on the North American continent.

Colourpoints have the same longhaired coat and the same large to medium-large physique as Persian cats. The shape of the head, legs, paws and tail are also unequivocal evidence of their relationship to Persians. Their Siamese heritage gives them their colour shadings and the markings on their coats.

Like Siamese cats, Colourpoints are born nearly white. The typical markings on the face, legs, paws and tail show up only later, as they mature, and they should be as evenly marked as possible. A good contrast between the markings and the basic body colour is also important.

Colourpoints come in many colour variations: with seal-coloured markings on a cream-coloured body, blue markings on a glacier-coloured body, chocolate markings on an ivory-coloured body, red markings on an apricot-coloured body and cream markings on a creamy white-coloured body. In addition there is a whole series of Tortie and Tabby variations. The standards lists a total of 20 colour variations.

Another trait inherited from the Siamese are Colourpoints' bright, shining deep blue eyes. Their character unites fine traits from both breeds: they are livelier and more frisky than Persians, affectionate, but not as boisterous and loud as Siamese. A Colourpoint is an ideal family cat in that this breed is quite amenable to children and other house pets.

The relationship between Colourpoints and Persians is unmistakable. They have their body colouring and their markings from the Siamese.

Semi-longhaired Cats

Birman: The Sacred Cat of Burma

There are many legends about the origin and past of the Birman, which is also called the Sacred Cat of Burma, because Buddhist priests supposedly kept them in their temples as holy cats. Today, however, it undisputed that the Birmans were bred for the first time in France in the 1920s and that the French gave the breed the exotic-sounding name of *sacre de Birmanie*.

The Birman's signature trait is short white gloves on the front paws and longer ones on the back paws. The Birman's coat is similar to that of the Colourpoint. This cat is a lovely housemate: gentle, devoted and affectionate.

A tale unquestionably from the realm of legends is one that tells of a priest who was attacked and killed by robbers as he worshipped the golden goddess Tsun-Kyan-Kse. As his white cat Sinh stepped onto the dead man and looked into the burning sapphires of the goddess's eyes, the deity's fiery glamour shone on the cat and gave it its signature golden-brown coat. Only the paws remained white, for they had been pressed into the dead man's body. Some interpret the white paws as a symbol of purity.

The white paws are the most conspicuous of the Birman's traits. On the front paws the white "gloves" should end in an even line straight across the paws, and on the back paws they cover the entire paw as a "gauntlet" and end on the back side of the leg exactly below the ankle joint. Aside from these white paws and a somewhat shorter coat, the Birman has a great deal of similarity to the Colourpoint. The Birman has an elongated and sturdy body, the head is broad and round with full cheeks, a medium-long nose without any indentation, a well-developed chin and round deep-blue eyes. The bushy tail is in proportion to the body. The Birman's legs and paws are short and powerful, and the coat is medium-long, silky and slightly curly on the stomach.

The body has a shimmering gold tone, and the markings on the head, tail and legs—like those on Siamese and Colourpoints—are seal-coloured, blue-grey, chocolate-coloured or blue. The kittens are born nearly white, developing their markings later. When the Birman is fully grown, the mask covers its entire face including the whisker pads and is connected to the ears by lines or tracings.

The coat of the Birman is not as long and thick as the coat of longhaired cats, so it doesn't mat as easily and is simpler to care for. Even a little trip outdoors won't harm this coat. Because these cats are very sensitive to the cold, however, they should only go outside when it is relatively warm. Regarding the character of the Sacred Birman, this cat lives up to the honour of its name. This is an intelligent and especially peaceful housemate with a gentle voice who is also friendly, devoted, affectionate and playful. The Birman greatly enjoys close contact with people and other cats. These are not a particularly good cats for families with small children, however, since they do not deal well with children's responses to cats and misunderstandings between the cats and children arise easily.

Turkish Van Cat

At the beginning of the 1950s a British tourist became acquainted with Van cats during her vacation in Turkey. She took a pair of them back to England with her, and later fetched three more cats. It took nearly two decades before the Turkish cats were recognised as a breed by the umbrella organisations of the noble cat breeder organisations. In the meantime, this cat has found enthusiasts not only in Europe, but in the USA and Australia as well.

The coat of the Van cat is long and silky and soft down to the very roots. Because there is no undercoat, the fur lies close against the body. The ideal Van cat is chalk-white without a trace of yellow. The cat's face is rusty red above the eyes and divided by a vertical white blaze. The large, tufted ears are set straight and fairly close together. They are white on the outside, as is the relatively long nose, while on the inside they are a delicate pink as are the nose leather and the paw pads.

Like the markings on the face, the tail is rusty red, and it is long, full and bushy. Some Van cats have rusty red spots called "thumbprints" irregularly distributed across their coat. Though they do not correspond to the ideal standard of beauty, these markings do not necessary lead to disqualification at exhibitions. The breeding of Van cats with creamy white markings rather than chestnut-brown ones is still relatively recent.

The body of the Van cat is medium-large, long and muscular. The legs are moderately long and their paws bearing small tufts of fur are especially delicate. This cat's large, oval-shaped light amber eyes with pink rims are very impressive. One occasionally sees Van cats with blue or different-coloured eyes, but these cats run the risk of being deaf, just like white Persians. Vans are known as intelligent, lively, curious cats and enjoy the occasional little adventures out into the garden. Since these cats are anything but afraid of water, they enjoy taking baths of the right temperature, but they must be thoroughly dried off afterwards. They are also very lively and especially devoted cats.

Information

Turkish cats are the refined descendants of the house cats that lived in south-eastern Turkey on Lake Van. They are thus also sometimes called simply Van cats. Their love of water is remarkable. They enjoy swimming and will sometimes even catch fish while swimming.

The Turkish Van is a strong cat and it loves water. The colourful facial markings between the eyes and ears are divided by a central white blaze.

Balinese

Balinese cats are not from the island of Bali, as their name might lead one to think. The cats of this relatively recent breed are in actuality longhaired Siamese cats. And that is what they were originally called. They owe their current name to their reputation for graceful movements, which call to mind the grace of a Balinese dancer.

This breed owes its origins to a whim of nature. Longhaired mutants had emerged earlier in the breeding of Siamese cats, but they were eliminated because they didn't correspond to the ideal standard of beauty. They were only bred when it occurred to American breeders in the 1950s that they could use the would-be mistake to continue breeding longhaired Siamese cats, violating all established rules. In the USA the longhaired Siamese or Balinese have been recognised as a distinct breed since 1970, and in Europe since the middle of the 1980s.

Balinese cats have the same long, slender physique as Siamese cats. Their wedge-shaped head and radiant, almond-

shaped blue eyes are also unequivocal evidence of their Siamese parentage. What sets them apart is their medium-long, fine and silky fur. Because these cats do not have the undercoat typical of longhaired cats, the coat lies flat against the body.

The colour variations are identical with those of the Siamese. The markings in the face and on the ears, legs, paws and tail should offer a clearly distinguishable contrast to the body colour.

Balinese have long, slender legs that are a little longer in the back than in front. They have delicate oval paws and a long, pointed and frequently quite bushy tail without any kinks, and their gait is especially graceful. The relatively large and pointed ears are set straight and well separated from each other, and the nose is straight and long. Balinese cats lend the impression of being intelligent and bright, and they enjoy playing without being as loud and boisterous as the Siamese.

The graceful Balinese have a slender physique and almond-shaped blue eyes. Their coat lies flat against the body because they have no undercoat, and it is easier to care for than the coats of other semi-longhaired cats.

Turkish Angora

The Turkish Angora is a cat with a long history. In the seventeenth century this cat arrived in France and England as a gift from Turkish sultans, but was displaced in the nineteenth century by the Persian cat and for decades was in danger of extinction. The zoo in its native region of Ankara (earlier Angora) made certain that this Turkish feline beauty was kept alive.

At the beginning of the 1950s a pair of Angoras came from the zoo in Ankara to the USA and the breed has been treasured by a growing number of cat enthusiasts ever since. In Europe the Turkish Angora was recognised as a breed only in the 1980s. While this cat was originally completely white, today it is bred in many colours and markings.

In contrast to its longhaired competitor, the Persian, the Turkish Angora has a long, limber body, long, slender legs and because of the absence of a thick undercoat, a coat that is substantially easier to care for. This coat is semi-long, fine, silky and wavy on longer body parts.

The comparatively small, wedge-shaped head and the long, straight nose also contribute to this cat's elegant appearance. The large, pointed ears are broad

The Turkish Angora is a slender, graceful cat with a semi-longhaired, silky coat and a bottle-brush tail.

at the base and frequently sport tufts of hair. Angoras' eyes are usually green or orange, medium-large and almond-shaped. White angoras often have blue or different-coloured eyes, which is again linked with the increased likelihood of deafness.

The Turkish Angora makes an altogether elegant and graceful impression with its muscular body, its long, pointed, bottle-brush tail and its delicate paws with tufts of fur on them. And the cat's nature is likewise gentle, cuddly, devoted and lively.

Somali

Because the Somalis, a relatively recent breed, are really longhaired Abyssinians, they were named for the country of Somalia, which is a neighbour to Ethiopia (formerly Abyssinia). Like other breeds, the Somali owes its existence to an originally unknown longhair gene that emerged in the breeding of Abyssinians, which was considered undesirable and kept quiet for a long time.

Somali cats were bred beginning only in the 1970s, first in the USA and then later in Europe as well. The longhaired relatives of the Abyssinians originally were found only in ruddy and agouti, but today the breed's accepted palette of colours is identical to the palette of its ancestor.

What distinguishes the Somali from the Abyssinian is not just the medium-long, extremely fine and thick coat, but also the substantially higher number of hairs with ticking. This ticking of the individual hairs shows the coat's colouring to particular advantage. The dark tips of the hairs should run as a shading along the spine to the tail. Ruffles and breeches, as the long fur around the neck and on

the back legs are called, are a desirable feature in Somalis.

Somalis are medium large, muscular and limber. Their moderate, wedge-shaped head shows slight rounding in profile. Their relatively large, cupped ears are set widely apart, stand straight up and have hair tufts. Their large, almond-shaped eyes are set far apart and they are very expressive. The eyes can be amber, hazelnut brown or green. They are framed by a light pair of "eyeglasses" and a short, dark, vertical "pencil stroke" that runs from lid and continues to the ear.

The legs of the Somali are long and slender, the paws oval and there are tufts of fur between the toes. The Somali's long, bushy tail is thicker at the base and pointed at the end. Somalis are lively cats, demanding lots of cuddling and playing.

In comparison to their ancestors, the shorthaired Abyssinians, Somalis have quite a long coat.

Norwegian Forest Cat

The Norwegian Forest Cat has a fascinating, wildcat-like appearance, which is more pronounced in the winter months. This cat is a true climbing and balancing artist.

The origin of the Norwegian Forest Cat remains largely obscure. For a long time this cat was found only in its native Nordic countries, where it has been bred since the 1930s. It has been recognised internationally only since 1977. With its long, bushy tail, this cat resembles the troll cats of Scandinavian fairy tales.

The Norwegian Forest Cat, known in her native region as *Norsk Skaukatt*, has a fascinating, wildcat-like appearance. The thick undercoat protects this cat from icy cold, and the smooth, slightly oily and water-resistant guard hairs repel rain and snow. This coat defends it against the raw climate of the far north.

The coat of the Norwegian Forest Cat first unfold its full magnificence when the cat is several years old, and even then only in winter. In summer and on exclusively indoor animals, the coat is shorter and softer, and the bib—which consists of a short collar at the neck, side mutton chops and frontal ruff—is less pronounced. There are no restrictions on acceptable colours and colour combinations. White markings, medallions and stomach patch all occur.

The head of the Norwegian Forest Cat has the form of an equilateral triangle from the base of the ears to the tip of the chin, with a medium-long straight nose. The large, slightly rounded ears are heavily furred and, as in the lynx, they are alert and pointed forward. The eyes of younger kittens are nearly round, later becoming large and almond-shaped. The eye colour should be harmonious with the basic colour of the coat.

Despite its length the coat is easily cared for. It should be brushed daily, and when

the coat is changing with the turn of seasons, it should also be combed daily.

The character of the Norwegian Forest Cast is not as wild as its appearance would lead one to believe; this is an exceptionally cuddly and gentle cat, toward children, too. Because these cats love the company of people and other cats, they should not be left alone, and they need an indoor climbing tree to give them sufficient opportunity to exercise their natural enthusiasm for climbing, balancing and cat acrobatics.

Maine Coon Cat

The Maine Coon is among the oldest and largest of the cat breeds. This cat's native region is the state of Maine in the chilly north of the USA, and 'coon is an informal version of the word racoon. This cat was probably given this name because of its bushy tail that resembles the racoon's tail. There is a fanciful and biologically impossible theory that this cat is the product of a crossbreeding between house cats and racoons. Even today, the origins of the Maine Coon remain unclear. It is assumed that short-haired American house cats bred with longhaired mutants brought from Europe by emigrants, traders and seafaring people. The Maine Coon's notable resemblance to the Norwegian Forest Cat leads to the speculation that they may have common ancestors.

It is documented that the Main Coon was shown at agricultural exhibitions in the nineteenth century and that the cat was prized as a rat and mouse hunter. From the original farm animal a rapidly recognised cat breed emerged. The breed's fame, however, didn't last very long.

As early as the turn of the century, when the first Persians arrived in the USA, the Maine Coon was gradually forgotten. For decades they were hardly ever seen at cat exhibitions. Only in the 1950s did the breed experience a comeback through the initiative of dedicated breeders and enthusiasts, and today it is popular throughout the world.

The bushy tail, which brings to mind a racoon, gave the Maine Coon its name. This breed is among the oldest and largest breeds of cats. The large, expressive eyes are especially impressive, as are the ample neck ruffle and the large, tufted ears and paws.

The Maine Coon is of grand size and weight. Since this cat is a late developer, its only fully grown at the age of three years. The angular-looking, long body is muscular with a broad chest. The legs are also powerful, and the paws are large and round with hair tufts. The tail, which is long like the body, is broad at the base and pointed at the tip and covered in long, flowing fur.

The primary trait in addition to the size of the body is this cat's heavy and shaggy but silky coat of differing lengths. The coat is especially long on the stomach and the back legs. Viewed from the back, the Maine Coon appears to sport knickers. From the front the cat's neck ruffle is visible. In relation to the body, the head is relatively small and square toward the muzzle. The medium-long nose appears snub in profile.

The large ears with tufts are broad at the base, are set high on the head far apart from each other and come to a point. The large, expressive eyes are slightly slanted, and also stand far apart. All shades of green, gold and copper are allowed in eye colour.

Because the fur has no undercoat, it rarely becomes matted and is easily cared for. The Maine Coon is in other regards an easy cat to care for, too, as long as one plays and cuddles with it sufficiently. This is an ideal family cat and gets along well with other house cats. There is one more trait that sets the Maine Coon apart from other cats: this cat doesn't just meow like everyone else, it makes unique chirping noises, which can indicate both contentment and its opposite.

Ragdoll

There is a very simple explanation for the name Ragdoll. Despite its imposing size, this cat feels especially relaxed when you gather one into your arms, and it enjoys cuddling, too. The first Ragdolls were born in California at the beginning of the 1960s, the children of a white longhair and a Birman. They have a powerful, broad, wedge-shaped head,

medium-long legs and paws with feathery tufts. The tail of the Ragdoll is long and bushy, and the notable feature of the face is full cheeks that taper toward the muzzle. The medium-large ears tip forward slightly at the base, are rounded at the top and tufted. The large, oval eyes are wide-set and usually blue in colour.

The coat of the Ragdoll is medium-long to long, thick, soft and silky. It lies against the body but moves along with the cat's every movement. It is longest around the neck and face, where it looks like a bib. The fur on the front legs should be short to medium-long and thick, but the fur on the back legs should be feathery. In winter the coat is thicker and longer than in summer. Dry or raw-looking fur, as well as matted fur, is judged as a flaw.

Ragdolls come in several pattern variations: bicolour, mitted and colourpoint, and the CFA includes a Van pattern as well. The bicolours have a white chest, stomach and legs with a dark face-mask, ears and tail. A signature trait of theirs is a white, symmetrical, inverted V on the forehead. The white gloves on the paws recall its Birman heritage. The breast, bib and chin are also white. Colourpoint Ragdolls have thoroughly coloured fur. The body colour should be a lighter tone than the points, but darker than the chest, bib and chin. The colour of the points should be well distinguished.

The Ragdoll enjoys affection and is very devoted. One can cuddle this cat as if it were a doll or a baby. The Ragdoll requires a lot of attention from its people and sufficient time for playing together.

Information *While the Ragdoll has a reputation for being especially insensitive to pain, this has recently been disputed. This cat is insensitive on its stomach, however, which is prone to becoming fat. The body should be long and muscular with a well-developed chest. The Ragdoll is fully grown only at three or four years of age.*

Ragdolls enjoy cuddling and despite their size will tolerate being held like a cloth doll.

Shorthaired Cats

Siamese

In contrast to many other breeds, the Siamese cat really does come from the country whose name it bears: Siam, which is now Thailand. This Far Eastern beauty with its elegant body form, graceful movements and radiant blue, almond-shaped eyes is one of the world's most beloved shorthaired cats.

The precise origins of the Siamese are obscure today. A drawing in a fourteenth-century volume of poetry indicates that there were already Siamese cats or cats similar to the Siamese that long ago. It is presumed that the Siamese emerged as a result of breeding between Thai house cats and Bengal cats. The first Siamese pair is reputed to have been brought to England by British General Consul Owen Gould around 1880. When Siamese cats were shown for the first time at an exhibition in London a few years later, their path to victory was assured. This cat became the darling of English society and was soon known and loved all over the world.

The standards of ideal beauty for the Siamese have changed, however, over time. In comparison to their earlier appearance, today's Siamese has a much more slender head, body and tail, and its eyes are more intense blue. The signature trait of this cat has nevertheless remained the same: the markings on the coat on the face, ears, paws and tail. While the first Siamese cats had only dark brown markings, there are now more than 20 colour varieties of this noble cat.

According to today's beauty standards, the Siamese must have a long, slim body

With its radiant blue eyes, graceful body and delicate movements, the Siamese cat is one of the most popular short-haired cats in the world. A distinctive trait of the Siamese are the pronounced markings on the face, ears, paws and tail.

No other cat has a voice as loud and penetrating as the Siamese.

The coat of the Siamese lies close to the body and is very short, fine-textured and glossy. It is important that any markings be well distinguished from the basic colour and that they form a good contrast to the body colour. At birth, Siamese cats are entirely white. Their final colours are only visible when full-grown. Overly slender Siamese cats with extremely narrow heads are especially susceptible to infectious diseases and dental problems. Siamese cats vary greatly from one another in character. They expect their people to interact with them intensively. They like to play, are lively and the most vocal of all cats. Their voice is loud and penetrating, which can lead to problems with neighbours in apartments with thin walls. Siamese cats are especially devoted and will allow themselves to be walked on a lead like a dog, but may react with great jealousy toward other people and cats.

with long, slender legs—slightly higher in the back than in the front—and small oval paws. The tail should be long, thin and taper to a point without any kinks. The head should be as well-proportioned as the body: wedge-shaped with a long, straight nose, a strong chin and rather large, wide-set pointed ears.

Siamese are born white and the typical colour markings on the coat appear only after a few months.

Opposite page: Prize-winning Siamese have a wedge-shaped head, and the large, wide-set ears form a straight line with the outline of the face.

Appearances are deceiving: Siamese cats can be very jealous of other cats.

Oriental Shorthair

The Havana, the eldest among the still young Oriental Shorthair Cats, is brown from hair root to tip like the renowned Cuban cigar tobacco. The coat of the black Oriental Shorthair, called Ebony, must also be evenly and thoroughly coloured.

The similarity between the Oriental Shorthair and the Siamese is unmistakable. The Oriental has the same slender body with long legs and the same characteristics, but without the coat markings typical of the Siamese. Single-coloured, tabby and spotted cats that result from a crossbreeding between Siamese and other shorthaired cats are called Oriental Shorthairs. In contrast to the Siamese, they have green eyes.

The oldest of the still relatively new breed of Oriental Shorthair is the Havana. The cat received this name because the colour of its coat resembles the renowned Cuban cigar tobacco. The coat has a uniform colouring in warm chestnut brown down to the hair roots. In addition to the Havana, there are also Oriental Shorthairs in lilac, white, black, blue, cinnamon, cream and caramel.

Among Oriental Shorthair tabbies, there is great variation in colour and pattern.

Slender, long-legged and exceptionally graceful, Oriental Shorthair cats with their wedge-shaped heads are similar to Siamese cats. Originally bred only as "single-coloured Siamese", these cats are increasingly popular in all their variety of colourings and coat markings.

The colours should be evenly distributed across the entire body and clearly distinguished from each other. This is also true of spotted and other striped Orientals, which usually have the typical M on their forehead.

Striped Orientals have closely spaced stripes running at right angles to the body. Spotted Orientals may have spots of various sizes, but they should not run together into a pattern of interrupted stripes. It is important that the pattern of spots be of uniform colour from the hair roots to the hair tips and that they offer a distinct contrast to the basic colour. The contrast between the spots and the basic colour is especially distinctive with brown, chocolate and red, and less so with blue, lilac and cream. The legs may have bars or be spotted. Light hair roots and white spots lead to loss of points.

Oriental Shorthairs otherwise have the same short, glossy coat close to the body as the Siamese. Their character is also very similar, though the Oriental Shorthair is generally more tolerant than the Siamese and not quite as demanding and loud, with a more melodic voice.

Burmese Cat

The Burmese is an exceptionally elegant cat with an exotic flair. The Burmese was purportedly worshipped as a holy animal by Buddhists priests in Burma, as were the Birmans. The names Birman and Burmese are easily confused, but the appearance of the two breeds have no similarities.

her with a dark brown Siamese cat. It took a few years for the strongly dominant Siamese character to weaken, but the result was the Burmese cat. The breed was recognised in 1936 in the USA, and in 1952 in England.

The standard demands that Burmese as a type have no visible similarity with either Siamese cats or with British Shorthairs. The medium-large and mus-

The powerful chest is typical of the Burmese cat, as are the large golden-yellow eyes and the fine, glossy coat, which in all colours is lighter on the stomach and chest than on the back.

Shorthaired cats such as the brown Burmese are visible in images on ancient Far Eastern manuscripts. The fact is that the ancestor of the Burmese was called Wong Mau and she was, in fact, from Rangun, the capital of Burma. Dr. Joseph Thompson, an American doctor, brought her back to California in 1930 and mated

cular body of the Burmese is rounded and has a powerful chest. The back is straight from the shoulder to the tail. The legs are long and slender, the paws delicate and oval. The medium-long tail is straight with a rounded tip. The head has broad cheekbones, is slightly rounded toward the top and wedge-shaped

Burmese cats were originally bred only in brown.

between gold and amber. Green eyes are considered a serious flaw in the Burmese.

The short, fine, satin-glossy fur of the Burmese should lie close to the body. The underside of the coat should be essentially lighter than the back and legs. The mask and ears are only somewhat darker than the body coat. In addition to the classic brown Burmese, this cat is now also found in blue, chocolate brown, lilac, red and cream. Torties may show coats with two colour tones of the basic colour. The colours may be mixed or may appear in spots.

More important to judges than the colour or markings of this cat, however, is the type of Burma, because they differ in several significant ways from American Burmese. According to the standards valid in the USA, Burmese cats have to be stockier altogether than in Europe, and they must have a rounded head as well as rounded eyes. The Tiffany cat, however, is largely identical with the European Burmese. The single difference between these two lies in the luxurious, long coat. Burmese characteristics are also prominent in the Burmilla. This cat emerged in the beginning of the 1980s as the result of a mating of a Burmese female and a Chinchilla male.

Burmese cats are especially sociable and very devoted, but they also have a powerfully developed will. They are not easily upset or frightened. While they get along with people very tenderly, they can be really brusque toward other cats.

Opposite page: The Burmilla has its origins in a mating between a Burmese mother and a Chinchilla father.

toward the bottom. The short nose has a distinctive kink. The ears, which are set well apart, are medium large and rounded at the corners. The eyes should be large and luminous, but neither round nor oriental. The eye colour varies

If a Burmese cat is to shine at exhibitions, it must not bear any visible evidence of its Siamese ancestry. Burmese cats are muscular and have a somewhat rounded head. Concerning their temperaments and their character traits, however, they are quite similar to Siamese cats. Burmese cats are happy to be able to play and wander about in the great outdoors.

Korat

The Korat is named for a province in its native Thailand, where the cat has been honoured for centuries as a bearer of good luck. The Thais call this cat "Si-Sawat", meaning luck and prosperity. With its silvery-blue shimmering coat, this cat has fans all over the world.

The beauty of the Korat is described in ancient Thai manuscripts. The first of these Southeast Asian cats came to the USA in the 1950s. The breed was recognised there in 1966, and in Great Britain in 1975.

The physique of the Korat resembles the curved back of the Siamese, but it is more muscular and powerful. The legs are medium long and slender. The medium-long tail has a rounded tip, and the heart-shaped head curves gently along the sides toward the muzzle. The large ears, set high on the head, have rounded tips and are curved at the base. The luminous green eyes are large and round. The short to medium-long blue coat, glossy and fine, lies very close to the body. The tips of the fur lend the coat a beautiful silvery shimmer that is especially distinctive in shorter coats. The silver tipping reaches its full intensity only when the cat is about two years of age. The nose leather and lips are dark blue or lavender, as are the paw pads, though these have an additional slight reddish tone. The coat of the perfect Korat has no shading and no tabby markings, nor does it have any white spots or areas.

Information

With their large, round eyes set in a heart-shaped face, Korats make a friendly and alert impression. And they are these things, too: lively, good-natured and loyal. They are often loathe to share their beloved people with other cats, however.

The Korat, which is considered a bringer of good luck in her native country, has large and luminous eyes.

British Shorthair

The British Shorthair is as varied in its physique, colours and markings as the ordinary house cat. In contrast to the normal kitty, however, the British Shorthair possesses a pedigree. Except for a few minimal differences, this cat is identical with the British and American Shorthairs. For lay people these differences are hardly noticeable.

Until the 1950s British Shorthairs were known as British Blues. They have a relatively strong body with a broad chest and somewhat short, powerful legs, round paws and a thick, medium-long tail with a thick base and rounded tip.

The head of the British Shorthair is round, with full cheeks and a distinctive chin. The nose is short, broad and straight. The small ears are rounded at the tips, are set far apart and are amply furred on the outside edge. The round eyes are wide-set and their colour varies according to the colouring of the coat. The coat must be short, dense and robust. Long or fluffy coats bring negative judgements. Single-colour British

The pedigree is what makes the most beautiful house cats into British Shorthairs. They show the complete variety of naturally beautiful coat markings and colours. With their muscular bodies on relatively short, sturdy legs, their dense coats and round heads, they are impressive evidence that house cats, too, have a breed.

Shorthairs come in white, black, chocolate, lilac, red, cream and blue (see the Chartreux). The coat should in any case be coloured as uniformly and thoroughly to the roots as possible. Chocolates are

allowed to have shadings and white markings. The tabby markings that frequently appear in young animals disappear over time. In fully grown single-colour British Shorthairs, tabby markings are considered a flaw.

The white British Shorthair can have blue, orange or different coloured eyes, and the nose leather and paws are pink.

The remaining single-coloured Shorthairs have eyes that are copper, orange or gold, and the nose leather and paws correspond to the colour of the coat.

The bicoloured British Shorthair has clear, distinct single-coloured spots. No less than one third and no more than half of the coat must be white. The coat colour of the tortoiseshell consists of a

mixture of black with dense and pale reds. The colours must be clearly separated from each other. White spots count as flaws. Only one short, narrow blaze on the face is allowed.

In a British Shorthair with classic tabby markings, the pattern be distinct, and the typical M has to mark the forehead. Above the M several lines run from the head to the shoulder markings. Seen from the top, it looks like the outline of a butterfly. From the "butterfly", an unbroken line runs continuously along the spine to the tail.

The spotted British Shorthair has the same pattern on its head. On the body and legs, the pattern consists of many oval, round, or rosette-shaped spots, all of which are clearly separated from each other and from the base colour. Silver-striped cats as well as those with black dots or black tipping have, in contrast to the rest of the British Shorthairs, green or hazelnut-coloured eyes.

The tipped British Shorthair has to have as white an undercoat as possible. Colourful tipping should be evenly distributed on the back, flanks, head, ears and tail and should achieve a sparkling effect. The colours of the nose leather and the paw pads must harmonise with the coat. Tipped cats that have tabby markings have no chance at prize-

winning. The same goes for smokes with a silver undercoat.

The characters and natures of the British Shorthair are as variable as with completely ordinary house cats. Like most shorthaired cats, these are quite full of temperament and playful. As a rule, the lighter the coat, the more sensitive the cat's reactions.

British Shorthair cats are found in countless variations: white with blue and orange eyes, black, blue-cream and, as on the opposite page, a silver-blotched tabby.

Information

The name Chartreux points to its French heritage. This cat has been shown since the earliest exhibitions, and remains especially popular in France. Its international break-through first took place after World War II. According to today's standards, the Chartreux is identical with the British Blue.

With its especially dense, slightly raised blue fur, the Chartreux might remind some people of an irresistible stuffed animal.

Chartreux belong to the category of British Shorthairs, but they form a special subcategory. The history of this plush blue cat can be traced back to the sixteenth century and is associated with many legends.

Carthusian monks apparently brought them from Africa to France and bred them in their monastery near Grenoble. According to legend, these cats were prized not only for their ability to catch mice in cellars and pantries, but also for their thick coats, which served as furs.

The coat of the Chartreux is as dense and sturdy as the coat of the British Shorthair, but it is even more plush. The Chartreux has an extra undercoat, lending it that additional thickness. The scale of colours ranges from light to medium blue. It is essential that the colour be uniform down to the hair roots. The coat of the fully grown cat may not show any

tabby markings, silver tipping or white. Like the coat, the nose leather and paw pads are blue.

The Chartreux is robust and is never bored, even in solitude. The cat is nevertheless more comfortable with company and gets along well with the entire family as well as with other cats. In contrast to its loud purring, this cat's meow is tentative, often hardly audible. With its even-tempered, peaceful, undemanding manner, the devoted Chartreux is a cat that feels comfortable both with single people and with families.

Russian Blue

At first glance the coat of the Russian Blue resembles the Chartreux, but the Russian Blue is fundamentally different from the British Shorthair in its much more slender and delicate physique.

Nothing is known about the origins of the Russian Blue with certainty. It is presumed that this cat was brought to England from the Russian port of Archangelsk because there was interest in the cat's coat. The cat was thus for a time called the Archangelsk cat. The Russian Blue was first shown in London in 1880.

The body of the Russian Blue appears long, slender and elegant. The legs and tail are long, and the tail ends in a point. The paws are small and oval. This cat's head is wedge-shaped and flat with a broad forehead and nose, a strong chin and a prominent muzzle. The almond-shaped, luminous green eyes are set far apart as are the large, pointed ears.

The most distinctive trait of the Russian Blue is its coat, which is short, dense, very fine and silky-soft. The coat is an evenly distributed blue colour and stands out from the body like a seal's coat. Because the coat is doubled, it shows a distinct silver shimmer. The coat of a fully-grown cat must show no tabby markings or shading.

To prevent the coat from lying too flat against the body, it should initially be brushed against the grain and only then brushed normally. The Russian Blue is a very adaptable cat that seeks and needs close contact with people.

Its silvery shimmering, plush coat lends the Russian Blue an especially noble appearance.

Abyssinian

More than any other kind of cat, the Abyssinian calls to mind depictions of Ancient Egyptian temple cats. The classic Abyssinian with its agouti coat resembles a miniature puma. Today Abyssinians are bred in eight different colours.

The similarity between the Abyssinian and the African Wildcat is no coincidence. The wife of a British officer brought one of these cats native to North Africa to England in the mid-nineteenth century. With this cat, whom she called Zulu, the breeding of Abyssinians began, and the breed was already recognised in 1882 in England. This is one of the few breeds of slender cats that was not crossed with the Siamese cat.

The Abyssinian has a medium-long, graceful, muscular body that appears very elegant. The tail is relatively long and ends in a point. The legs are also long and slender. The head is slightly wedge-shaped with a slightly curved, medium-long nose. In profile the head shows a gentle slope toward the forehead. The relatively large, cup-shaped ears have hair tufts, are wide-set and stand straight up. The large, almond-shaped eyes are green, amber or hazelnut-coloured and with their dark outlining are particularly expressive.

The characteristic trait of the Abyssinian, however, is the short, close-lying coat with double to quadruple ticking, that is, several distinct bands of colour on each hair. This ticking gives the coat its attractive, constantly changing shading. The ticked hairs are distributed evenly across the whole body without any patterns of stripes or spots. This classic agouti colouring is more pronounced in the Abyssinian than in any other breed of cat.

The agouti Abyssinian has a golden-brown body colour ticked with black and a reddish-orange or apricot-coloured undercoat colour. The sorrel Abyssinian has a copper-red body hair colour with

On the opposite page: Sorrel is one of the classic Abyssinian colours. Typical of all Abyssinians is the fine, close-lying coat with fur that has several colours on each strand of hair, which is called ticking.

Double to quadruple ticking is responsible for the multicoloured shimmering of the Abyssinian coat.

are also headstrong. They do not tolerate teaching or training; they make it clear that they train their people. Initially they may be somewhat reluctant to trust people, but once they have made friends, these cats are especially devoted and loyal.

chocolate-coloured ticking and an apricot undercoat. The blue Abyssinian has a blue-grey coat with steel-blue ticking, with a cream or light beige undercoat. Abyssinians move very gracefully, they are very full of temperament and they

Agouti Abyssinians bear a resemblance to small pumas and call to mind depictions of Ancient Egyptian temple cats like no other breed of cat. With its slender, muscular body, graceful movements and characteristic ticking, the Abyssinian is an extraordinarily elegant cat.

95

Manx

The Manx differs from all other cats in one essential way: the Manx has no tail. The cat did not acquire this trait through breeding: this cat is naturally tail-less and has lived for hundreds of years on the Isle of Man in the Irish Sea, where some people speak the Celtic language Manx. Various legends offer differing explanations for the Manx's lack of a tail.

The most distinctive trait of the Manx is the tail, which is either missing entirely or only a stump.

One tells that dogs are supposed to have bitten off the tail as they all left Noah's ark. According to other legends these cats came from Japan with Phoenician merchants, or they swam ashore on the Isle of Man when a Spanish ship of war ran aground. So much for the legends. The fact is that this is a hereditary defect which presumably arose as a result of many years of inbreeding. In the Manx breed, there are rumpies and there are stumpies. While the rumpy is entirely tailless and has a hole in place of a tail, the stumpy has a stump of a tail. The taillessness and physique of the Manx leads not only to the typical Manx hopping, rabbit-like gait, it can also lead to health problems.

According to the standard, Manx cats should be altogether compact and round: they have a round head with a rounded muzzle, plump cheeks and large, round eyes as well as a short back that runs in the form of an arch from the shoulders to the curved rump, and the rump should be higher than the shoulders. The standard demands the absolute absence of any tail. At the end of the spinal column, where a tail would otherwise be, neither bones nor cartilage should be detectable. The coat is doubled and should feel like soft upholstery. The undercoat is dense and shorter than the overcoat. Colour and markings play only a minor role in the judging of this cat. All patterns except Siamese patterns are allowed.

Almost identical to the tail-less Manx cat is the Cymric. The single trait that distinguishes the Cymric from the Manx is the medium-long coat that gradually becomes longer from the shoulders toward the back.

Because a cat's tail is not merely decorative for them, but a vital aid in balance and movement, all Manx and Cymric cats are poor climbers and to some extent have difficulty standing and walking, as well. Manx and Cymric cats are considered to be intelligent and especially devoted.

Scottish Fold

The physique of the Scottish Fold is largely similar to that of the British Shorthair cat. This cat has distinctive ears, however, which are folded forward and downward, lending the cat an original appearance and clearly distinguishing the Scottish Fold from other cats.

Cats with folded ears are supposed to have been sighted 200–300 years ago in China and were thus designated China cats. Their existence was often doubted until farm cats with truly folded ears were discovered in Scotland in the early 1960s, and then in other countries as well. The breeding of folded-ear cats began with these first discoveries.

According to standard, the body of the Scottish Fold should be well-rounded and look well-nourished. The tail should be long and agile, ending in a point. The plump-cheeked head and rounded muzzle, powerful chin and jaw all contribute to a general impression of roundness in this cat. Males are allowed to have truly chubby cheeks. The head blends into a short neck. The eyes are large and round, separated by a broad nose-bridge with a small and slightly bent nose. The colour of the eyes must suit the coat, in which all the colour variations of the British Shorthair are allowed.

Naturally, there are strict, established standards for the ears. They should be small and rounded toward the top and folded both forward and downward, the tighter the better. They should lie on the head like a cap, thus underscoring the round appearance of the face. The greatest number of points are granted for the appearance of the ears. Folded ears are unequivocally an abnormality that in the opinion of veterinarians easily leads to ear infections and can impair hearing—one of the most important senses for a cat. The Scottish Straight has the very same ancestor cat as the Scottish Fold and is otherwise identical to it, but the Scottish Straight does not have folded ears. According to the standard, this cat has medium-large, slightly rounded ears. The inside base of the ears points slightly inward and the outer tip lines up with the rounded contour of the head. There is also a longhaired variant of the Scottish Fold. All these variations have the same physique and the same type of character, all love cuddling and are very playful.

The Scottish Fold is recognisable at first glance from its ears, which are folded forward and downward once or even twice. The coat has a similar number of colour variations and markings as the British Shorthair.

Rex Cat

The Rex cat has a quite unique coat that explicitly distinguishes this cat breed from all others: the coat is naturally curly, wavy and crimped. The cat who gave his curly coat to his heirs and who thus created a new breed in the world of cats was called Kalibunker.

It was a woman farmer in British Cornwall who made the curly-furred animal into the ancestral father of all Rex cats. In 1950 she discovered the cat in the litter of a white tortoiseshell mother. Because she knew the curly hair of the Rex breed of rabbit, Kalibunker became a Rex cat.

Since more cats with curly hair later turned up and were bred in other regions, the Rex cat from Cornwall was named Cornish Rex. Then came Devon Rex from Devonshire, German Rex and Rex Oregon in the USA. The youngest breed to join the Rex cats is the Poodle Cat, which was first bred in Germany. Cornish Rex is slender and muscular, has long, straight legs, a long tail ending in a point and covered with curly fur. The head is wedge-shaped and tapers into a powerful chin. In profile, the face forms a straight line from the middle of the forehead and fades into the tip of the long nose. The large ears, which are set high on the head are wide at the base, rounded at the tips and covered with fine fur. The colour of the oval, medium-large eyes should harmonise with the colour of the coat, and the long whiskers and eyebrows should also be wavy.

The Cornish Rex is judged for its coat, which should be curly, short, fine, soft and crimped — curly, wavy and crimped in particular on the back and tail. All coat colours are permitted, as is asymmetrical white marking. The only pattern not permitted in the Cornish Rex is the Siamese pattern. Bald spots, shabby fur and overly short fur as well as a short or bald tail are all considered flaws.

Concerning the coat, the Cornish Rex and German Rex are very similar, but the physique and head shape of the German Rex correspond more to the British Shorthair. The physique is more powerful and the head is rounder. The body of the Devon Rex is slender, firm and muscular, and its legs are bowed. This cat's head with its full cheeks calls the Burmese to mind. The large, oval-shaped eyes are placed far apart, and the large ears are set relatively low. The coat is as short and soft as on other Rex cats, but the Devon Rex coat consists of some ordinary overcoat fur, and this fur is not as pronounced in it waviness.

The Rex coat is exceptionally easy to care for. It requires neither combing nor brushing, but needs only to be lightly wiped with a damp cloth or chamois. Rex cats are playful, very devoted and affectionate.

The Devon Rex has extremely large ears.

The coat of the Cornish Rex below right is wavier.

Opposite: The body of the German Rex is more powerful and the head is rounder.

Japanese Bobtail

The Japanese Bobtail has been around for centuries in its native country. As the name suggests, this cat's signature trait is a shortened tail, which occurs in several different variations.

The Bobtail can be seen on countless ancient Japanese pictures and drawings. The tri-colour brindled Bobtail is considered an especially lucky cat, and this one is called "Mi-Ke" by the Japanese. This cat's short tail is not a deformity. Superstitious Japanese are of the opinion that only cats without tails or with short tails are good. Long tails in their eyes bring bad luck.

The body of the Japanese Bobtail is long, slender and elegant but also powerful and muscular. The legs are also long and slender, and the paws are medium-large and oval. The typical tail is short, covered in long fur and resembles a tassel, but tails also vary greatly from cat to cat. The tail must be clearly visible and is composed of one or more curves, angles, or kinks. The furthest extension of the tail bone from the body should be no longer than fourteen centimetres. The direction in which the tail is carried is also not important.

The head of the Japanese Bobtail is shaped like an equilateral triangle. The large, oval eyes are set at a slight slant, and the ears are large and upright. A short, round heat and a short body are both judged as flaws.

The coat of the Japanese Bobtail is medium-long, soft and silky. All the colour variations that are allowed for British Shorthairs are permitted for this cat as well with the exception of the Siamese markings and Abyssinian agouti. The tri-colour "Mi-Ke" in black, red and white is especially popular.

The Japanese Bobtail has a friendly character and a relatively delicate voice, of which the cat makes frequent and cheerful use.

The fan-shaped short tail of the Japanese Bobtail resembles a tassel with its fur.

The Cat Home

Cats enjoy their favourite places, all nice and cosy on a blanket or an old towel.

What Cats Need to be Happy

Cats are modest creatures as far as the furnishing of their home is concerned: a basket with a soft lining, a litter tray, feeding and water bowls, a scratching post, cat grass and a table-tennis ball to play with suffice. If in addition there are dear people around who cuddle and play with the cat, their every wish is met.

The cat home should be completely set up before your velvet-pawed housemate moves in. It is also important that you allow yourself sufficient time to make the cat's move and settling in period as comfortable and easy as possible. Single people who work outside the home should ideally plan a few vacation days, since the groundwork for a harmonious life together are established in the first few days a cat is with its new owner.

Kittens should be at least ten weeks old before they are separated from their mothers. It is ideal for the cat to meet you and perhaps even to have become friendly with you before the move. This makes the separation from the kitten's accustomed environment easier. Lastly, keep in mind that young kittens were used to frolicking about with their siblings and that they suddenly have to negotiate an unfamiliar environment. As compensation they require a lot of petting and attention from a two-legged companion, particularly in the first few days. But it is by no means just young kittens who require plenty of time to cuddle and play to settle in comfortably at a relatively quick pace. The adjustment for an older cat suddenly removed from its familiar surroundings is much more difficult. In this situation it is particularly helpful if you take some familiar

and beloved object along with you: a cushion from a favourite lounging spot, a ball to play with or even the litter tray the cat was used to. If the cat then also senses your love, it will soon forget its old home and appreciate its new one.

Older cats in particular, however, should be allowed sufficient time for adjustment; don't pet them or carry them against their will. Forced affection has the opposite effect. Calmly await the time when the cat brushes up against your legs of its own will, thus communicating its desire for friendship and closeness.

Immediately upon arrival, show the cat where the litter tray is located. The cat may make use of it right away, but will probably first investigate the rest of its new environment, which cats generally prefer to do on their own. During the first tour of discovery, however, you

should not allow the cat to wander out of your sight, and you should pay particular attention that all windows and balcony or terrace doors are closed.

All cats, young and old, adjust to their new environment quickly when they sense genuine affection in the people around them. It is only a matter of time before they begin to communicate a desire for petting and affection, to cuddle up contentedly and to purr with satisfaction.

107

Any balconies in your home and the garden must initially be taboo. Cats should only be allowed outdoors after they feel properly at home in a new location, two weeks at the earliest. As soon as the kitten has finished its tour of the house and its curiosity has been satisfied, it will be very happy to find its favourite food in its food bowl. If the new cat then curls up near you or even on your lap and begins to purr, you can look forward to many satisfying years together.

Safe Transportation

There are circumstances in which a former owner gives up kittens or an older cat only reluctantly, and because of their strong attachment to the animal will deliver it personally to its new home. If

A basket or a plastic travelling container with a latching door will ensure that your kitten does not escape along the way to its new home out of fear and nervousness. With the cat carrier placed securely on the back seat, the kitten will safely survive its first trip in the car.

this is not the case and you pick up your cat yourself from a private home, an animal shelter or a breeder's house, you will need a container in which you can transport the cat safely so that it does not try to escape.

For its first journey in a car, a cat should have a companion to calm and stroke the cat, who may be nervous or even whimpering. Under no circumstances, however, should you remove the cat from the container. This could endanger the life of the kitten and of the people in the car, too, since some cats genuinely panic and may interfere with the driver's ability to handle the vehicle.

The travelling container can be a plastic cat carrier or a sturdy basket with a cover, but in any case it should close and latch securely and be large enough to allow for the cat's fully-grown size. After all, you will be using the cat carrier in the future, for example, for trips to the veterinarian. A cat carrying basket has one advantage over plastic carriers in that your cat might well enjoy curling up inside it at home, too.

Those who have little experience dealing with cats should have the previous owner show them just how to pick up and hold a kitten properly—never at the neck! This grip is reserved for feline mothers, and even cats use this hold only until the kittens reach a certain age. The neck grip can easily lead to internal injuries. This is the right method: lay one hand on the cat's belly between the front legs and use the other hand to hold the bottom of the cat, giving support to the back legs and hind quarters.

By no means should you ever force a cat into the cat carrier. Wait calmly until the cat goes in its own out of curiosity. Gentle speaking and a yummy treat can work wonders.

Ask the previous owner about the cat's habits and quirks, and be sure to ask about the cat's favourite food. You should have enough of this food for at least the first few days. You will immediately gain in standing with your new cat, and you won't need to fear that the cat will not eat. The way to a cat's heart is through the stomach.

Those who have little experience with cats should learn the proper way to hold a cat. The neck grip, below, is reserved for cat mothers alone: when people try this it can lead to internal injuries. Even mother cats use this grip only until the young are able to run on their own.

That Private Place

Young kittens learn cleanliness from their first days. In the beginning, they are cleaned by their mothers.

A perfect example of cleanliness was our little Filou, a completely ordinary house cat. Although she whined for the entire three-hour car ride home and disdained the tray filled with litter, she didn't have

any accident. She just stepped over the threshold of her new home and directly into the cat box.

A cat box that is always filled with clean litter is an essential even for a cat who goes outside. New designs for cat boxes are continually being produced, but an ordinary plastic tub is perfectly sufficient, as long as it cannot be knocked over easily and has sides that are low enough for the cat to step over them comfortably. Cat boxes with covers are less popular with most cats because they feel constricted by them and because they are disturbed by the odours that get trapped inside them.

The litter tray should be in a quiet area, since cats prefer to "do their business" undisturbed and unobserved. It must be easily accessible and available to the cat at all times. The best place is generally a bathroom or toilet. The cat box should be filled with litter 3 to 5 cm deep. The least expensive litter is made of peat, sawdust or paper strips, but these have the drawback of easily getting stuck in the cat's paws and fur. Industrially produced litter, which consists of finer or coarser grains, is more hygienic. Because this litter also absorbs moisture and odours, it doesn't require changing quite as often. Even with commercial litter, how-

Information

Cleanliness is a trait that cats are, generally speaking, born and raised with. If a kitten is not separated from its mother prematurely, it is usually litterbox trained by the time it moves to its new home.

A cat does not like to be observed while "doing its business". It carefully buries all traces. It is essential that the cat box always be filled with clean litter.

The Cat's Table

It is best to set your cat's "table" in a quiet corner of the kitchen. If you serve the cat its meal on a washable mat, you can save yourself the trouble of sweeping and mopping up after every meal. Most cats are in the habit of first grabbing a small pile of food out of the bowl for themselves and only then eating it. Cats do not like to have their meals in continually changing locations, so it is best to keep the bowls in one certain place.

All cats require two bowls: one for food and one for water. They should be difficult to knock over and easy to wash. Cats find cleanliness important here, too, besides the fact that crusted bits of leftover food are neither hygienic nor healthy. Even if they are very hungry, cats will not eat from dirty dishes. Be certain to keep a bowl filled with water at all times. If you have the impression that your cat is drinking too little, try to place the water bowl somewhat farther away from the food dish.

There are special food bowls for cats made from all sorts of materials and in all kinds of shapes and colours, and there are even automatic feeding bowls with battery-operated timers and built-in

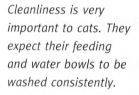

Even outdoor cats who are allowed to roam freely outside need a clean litter tray at home.

ever, tiny remnants of the litter will inevitably get stuck in the paws and be tracked throughout the house.

How often the litter must be changed varies greatly from cat to cat. The litter tray must never be allowed to smell bad, and it should be rinsed out before each refill with fresh litter. Do not pour the old litter into the toilet, because it will lead to clogging. This does not include the wet clumps or piles, which should be removed once or twice daily with a little shovel. Your cat will thank you by not having accidents in your house.

Cleanliness is very important to cats. They expect their feeding and water bowls to be washed consistently.

coolers, inventions of which presumably only few cats approve.

Whether you choose bowls made of plastic, ceramic or glass is in principle unimportant. If you have a kitchen floor made of tile or another hard material, plastic bowls are more advisable. They do not rattle as loudly when cats push the bowl back and forth through the room because they do not care for the food in it.

Finally, cats expect not only that their food be served in clean bowls, but also that it be served rather punctually. Their inner clocks send them to their food bowls at approximately the same time every day.

Cats clean their muzzles and paws carefully after eating.

People can only dream of having the daily rhythm of a cat. A cat sleeps and rests for more than half of the day—and not necessarily just in their own little basket.

Space for Cuddling

Cats sleep for more than nine hours daily, and they spend nearly as much time in drowsy rest and cleaning—and at all hours of the day and night. One favourite habit is the little nap after mealtime, during which they are most displeased if they are disturbed. Hence the expression "catnapping". The imaginations of producers of cosy sleeping places for cats seems to be almost inexhaustible. There is nothing that isn't made: cushy telephone boxes, rubbish bins, mice, etc. Many a cat enthusiast has determined, however, that such amusing purchases often turn out to have been money spent in vain and that their cat is often happier sleeping and resting in an old cardboard box.

Because cats decide on their own resting spots and don't let anyone else tell them where or when to take their naps, at first you should not invest too much in a sleeping spot. The cat carrier or a very ordinary basket is completely sufficient in the beginning. These places need to be large enough, though, so that the cat can stretch itself out fully in them, even when the cat is fully grown. A soft cushion with a removable and washable

A Cat's Day

Sleeping	Resting	Playing	Cleaning	Strolling and Walking
9 h 40 m	5 h 20 m	3 h 40 m	3 h 40 m	1 h 40 m

cover or a woollen blanket are the best choices for lining the cat's basket. Place the basket in a quiet corner that doesn't get a lot of traffic, but don't ban it to a dark corner. Cats like to experience what's happening around them even while they're sleeping and resting.

Cats prefer to find sleeping spots that are up high so that they can observe their surroundings without any obstacles. Your cat will always occasionally find new sleeping spots, though, whether it be an armchair that you especially favour, a basket of freshly ironed cloth-

clean themselves and observe birds, people, cars, etc. in peace. Be careful, though, that this doesn't cause a draft and that the windows are closed. If you have windows that can be tipped outward from the top, beware: tipped windows can become extremely dangerous traps for cats. A dosing cat who suddenly notices a bird flying past may get caught and break its neck in a tipped window.

No matter how cosy a kitty basket is, a cat is likely to find other favourite places for resting, too. For dosing, in particular, cats prefer elevated perches. This lets them observe everything happening in their environment.

ing, or a shelf in a closet, a bookcase or a sideboard. At night, they will often enjoy sleeping curled up at your head or feet. Another favourite spot for curling up are dining room chairs, as long as the tablecloth hangs low enough to hide them. And almost every cat loves to nap on windowsills, where they can rest,

Scratching and Climbing

If your cat lives indoors and has no opportunity to sharpen its claws outside, you must provide it with an appropriate substitute from the first day onward. Otherwise you will discover the traces of your beloved kitty's claws very quickly on your upholstered furniture, walls and carpets.

Scratching boards and posts and trees are available in all sorts of designs and for a wide range of prices, from a simple board that attaches to the wall to a luxurious, ceiling-high scratching and climbing tree with different platforms and cubby holes. If you have a knack for carpentry, of course, you can build your own scratching post or, better yet, find a natural tree trunk with a bit of bark and

Cats sharpen their claws by scratching.

a legged base to screw onto a board, and you can even attach a board to the top of it as a perching spot.

To prevent the scratching and climbing post from shaking and sliding, place an anti-slip mat under the base and position the post near a wall. These precautions will prove their worth. If a cat has even a single bad experience with a scratching post, she will avoid it in the future and instead use your furniture, wallpaper or carpeting for sharpening. A scratching post not only lets cats sharpen their claws on it, they climb on it as well.

A simpler and more economical alternative, though not quite as effective, is to attach a scratching board to the wall at an appropriate height. This, too, you can easily make yourself by gluing carpeting or tatami matting to a board. Or you can offer your cat a densely-woven natural fibre mat for sharpening its claws.

All is well in the world of a cat who has a post for scratching, climbing and playing.

117

The Toy Chest

Playing is one of the favourite activities of any cat, and cats aren't picky about what constitutes a toy. What matters is that the toy move. Before you buy toys, look around for inspiration in your household first. You won't believe the paraphernalia you will be able to find that is suitable for playing with your cat, with the emphasis purposely on playing *with* your cat. Playing is fun for your cat only when you play, too. The daily hour of play is a must for anyone who adopts a kitten. Before your feline friend even arrives at your house, collect empty spools of thread, corks, tissue paper and little sticks. This will already give you a sufficient supply of toys for the first few days and play sessions. With time you'll discover new opportunities to set up even more varied ways of playing with your cat. Variation is a must to keep things interesting, because playtime should never be a boring obligation for you or for your cat.

Cats love balls of wool, but they can also easily get tangled up in them.

One essential element of your toy collection should be a table-tennis ball, or better yet several, since these little balls have a way of disappearing and then miraculously reappearing during a thorough cleaning or even when moving house. Objects with sharp corners are

not suitable as toys, since cats can easily hurt themselves on them. Small objects such as marbles, beads or buttons are inappropriate because they can be swallowed.

Unfortunately, danger lurks in many fun potential "toys". Small balls of crumpled up aluminium foil are not a good choice

since they can damage your cat's teeth. The renowned ball of wool is a potential danger, especially for young kittens, as they can easily become entangled in the yarn. And those wonderfully crinkly plastic bags can also become a seriously dangerous trap, because little cats like to crawl into them and then sometimes have trouble finding their way back out. Beyond these concerns, the only limits

Playing is among cats' favourite activities, and not just young cats. Anything that moves, rolls or flies can be a suitable toy.

When cats cannot nibble on grass in the garden, you have to provide a substitute in the home. A pot with cypress grass or special pre-sown cat grass boxes are both options.

are those of your own imagination. Anything that rolls, runs or flies is of interest. Little balls of rustling tissue paper make wonderful toys, as do walnuts, little bits of fur and short sisal cords with a knot for feline hunting tied at one end. Hide-and-seek is a splendid game, and to play this all you need to do is cut a pair of spy-holes into a cardboard box.

To give your cat the opportunity to play when you are not home or when you are not available to play, tie a toy mouse, a cork or a little cloth ball to the end of a sisal cord and hang it securely from the ceiling or the scratching post so that the end dangles just above the ground.

Grass for Nibbling

Just like people, cats need to eat greens, though for very different reasons. While people require leafy foods for their nutrients, grass helps cats get rid of hair swallowed during grooming. If your cat has no way of nibbling on grass, you must offer a substitute. This is especially important for longhaired cats.

Not surprisingly, a good deal of fur ends up in a cat's stomach as a result of their daily cleaning, and the strands form little balls there. The technical term for these hairballs is *bezoars*. So that the indigestible hair doesn't have a negative impact on cats' health, they have to vomit them out of their system. Grass naturally furthers this process by irri-

tating the stomach and stimulating the urge to vomit.

The substitute meadow can consist of a flowerpot on the window sill or a crate on the balcony. Grass seeds, oats and wheat are all suitable seeds for cat grass. Since the "meadow" quickly becomes unsightly because of the nibbled tips and the new crop requires time to sprout, you should always have a well-timed second crop growing.

An alternative to planting seeds oneself is to buy special pre-sown cat grass boxes. Or you can buy a pot of cypress grass: cats are wild about it and it is also a decorative plant. Providing your cat with sufficient greenery to nibble on reduces the chances that it will nibble on your houseplants. Beside the fact that nibbled houseplants do not look so attractive, some of them also present a danger to the health of your cat.

Cats eat grass to help them vomit up fur swallowed in grooming.

Fresh Air

Cats enjoy fresh air, too. If you have an indoor cat who enjoys sitting on the windowsill, it is a good idea to outfit the window with a screen. This allows you to comfortably open the window and let in fresh air without having to worry that the cat might escape or fall out, which is not as harmless an event as many think. Tipping windows should have a latch that prevents the window from slamming shut.

The garden is a paradise for cats only when there is no danger from neighbours or bird watchers who dislike cats, pesticides, dogs and passing cars. Only rarely can a garden be sufficiently secured so

contains much for young
kittens to explore, they
also take in lots of
healthy fresh air. At first
the little ones should
get accustomed to their
periods out of doors
only under supervision.

that a cat will stay only in its own territory. This would require, for example, a
two-metre high chain-link fence with the
top section slanted in toward the garden.
But even this is not an insurmountable
obstacle for especially gifted climbers
and jumpers. Another alternative is the
type of electric fence that is used in
agriculture.

The danger that cats pose to birds is
exaggeratedly high in the minds of many

people. Only very young birds and elderly, sick birds are really in any danger
from a house cat. The chances that a cat
will catch a fully grown, healthy bird are
minimal, so it is not necessary to put a
collar with a bell around the neck of a
cat. It does not serve the birds any purpose, and it harms the cat. The continuous tinkling sound makes cats nervous and aggressive, since they have an
acute sense of hearing.

You should allow your cat to have its
first adventure out of doors only after
two to four weeks in your home and
initially only under supervision. Have

your cat become accustomed early on to
wearing a collar with an identification tag
with your name, address and telephone
number. The collar should be neither too
narrow nor too wide, so that the cat cannot strangle itself while prowling around
in the bushes or climbing. Collars with
an elastic insert are ideal.

If you want to let your cat outside on its
own whenever and as long as it wants,
then a cat door is worth the investment.
The upper edge of the door is hinged so
that your darling can walk in or out at
any time. Since one can never be certain,
however, that outdoor cats will always
return, it is advisable to have your cat
tattooed or tagged with a microchip and
registered with a lost-and-found registry
as soon as it is fully grown. For this you
will need photos of your cat. Photos also
prove useful if your cat goes missing and
you have to search the neighbourhood.
Someone might be able to remember
having seen your four-legged friend, and
that is more likely to happen if they can
glance at a photo than if they have only
vague descriptions.

*Cats who are great
climbers and jumpers
should be trained early
on to wear a collar with
a name and address tag
on it, since they rarely
remain in their own
garden. The constant
tinkling of even a tiny
bell attached to the
collar to warn birds
taxes a cat's fine sense
of hearing.*

Getting Adjusted to Each Other

Top Cat Names

Just like any child, a cat needs a name. Whether the cat recognises the name is another matter, but that has less to do with ability than with will. Sometimes

Even a name that sounds lovely to cat ears is no guarantee that a kitty will actually come when called.

cats do not care to listen. If a cat were to choose a name for itself, it would decide to give itself a two-syllable name that has two vowel-sounds in it such as "oo", "ah" or "ee". These sounds are particularly pleasing to cats' ears. So if you choose Misty or Morris, Sophie or

Sooty, you can assume that your velvet-pawed one will enjoy hearing its name. Additional names that are popular for cats include Casper, Charlie, Felix, Lucy, Max, Missy, Morris, Oliver, Oscar, Sam, Simba, Smokey, Tigger and Toby.

Morris, Tigger and Fluffy have it a little better than cats with ugly-sounding names. If your cat is a regular little rascal, you might name it Oscar. If it's especially curious, you could name the cat Francis after the cat detective in the novel *Felidae*. Even pedigree cats with a impressive but unpronounceable names usually don't object to being renamed. The only limits are the bounds of your own imagination, and if your imagination could use a boost, try this website: http://www.kittynames.com

The earlier you christen your little kitty the better the chances that the cat will actually listen and respond to its name. Address the kitten by name at every opportunity, especially when cuddling and petting, during play at during mealtime. If Pussy really comes as soon as you call, then she naturally deserves a reward. But you can probably count on having to wait at least a few weeks for this, and it may not work at all. As any veteran cat person can tell you, a cat does not respond to commands, but only if it wants to.

The Sixth Sense

In their ability to perceive things, cats are a step ahead of human beings. While we have to make do with just fives senses, cats have a sixth sense that makes them hypersensitive to danger. Cats perceive every little change in their environment, however slight, and that has given them the reputation of having clairvoyant abilities.

To this day in Morocco, for example, you will find no one who will kick a cat. Cats are credited with having saved the lives of many people during the major earthquake at Agadir in 1960. Meowing loudly,

their sensitive paw pads, sense pre-shocks that are imperceptible to humans. This ability is not limited to earthquakes, however. In other major kinds of catastrophes, as well, including wildfires, leaking gas and defective ovens, cats are said to have contributed to the fact that people were able to get to safety in time because they were warned by the cats' unusual behaviour.

Cats' eyes, which allow them to see six times as well as humans, have always had a fascinating effect on people. It is only a rumour, however, that cats are able to see in the dark. On the other hand, they are able to see in what strikes us as complete darkness. Cats' eyes reflect light in the darkness with the help of a special layer of cells at the back of their retinas, called the *tapetum lucidum* (Latin for "bright carpet"). This shiny layer of cells, acting like a mirror, reflects light back to the retina's cells and makes certain that every bit of light

Cuddling has to be learned. Like a small child, a person must learn to understand "cat language" in order to know how to respond.

the cats left their houses before the earthquake had fully destroyed the city. The people who followed them survived. Similar stories circulated in Yugoslavian Skopje, too, where there was an earthquake in 1963, and in other areas as well. Researchers believe that cats, with

Cats rely not merely on five senses the way people do. Their sixth sense allows them to sense major catastrophes before they happen, and this has saved the lives of many people. They also have a very acute sense of time. Their internal clock determines the structure of their day.

127

Cats' eyes are fascinating both because of the way they look and because they can see when human eyes perceive nothing but complete darkness. With their large, upright ears, cats perceive noises that no person and not even a dog can hear. Even their sense of smell is significantly better developed than ours. Kitties can get genuinely "drunk" from certain odours.

Information

Cats' eyes can distinguish between the colours red, green and blue. In over 2,000 experiments at the Institute for Zoology at the University of Mainz, cats had to choose between yellow and blue to get their food. Ninety-five per cent of the cats chose blue, even when the lighting level was changed. Red is generally considered to be the cat's favourite colour.

available is used. A cat's eye, then, has the ability to adapt continuously to changing light conditions and thus resembles a camera's aperture or a set of mini-blinds. In increasing darkness, the same pupils that are slits in the daytime become as round as saucers.

Cats' eyes are fascinating not just because of the way they work, but also because they're interesting to look at. Cats' eyes, with their slight slant and their green colour, are widely considered a symbol of beauty, hypnotic and mysterious at the same time. Perhaps women have also been inspired by the distinct lines around the eyes of many breeds of cats. At birth, by the way, all cats have blue eyes. Their later colour develops only in the course of the first three months of life. White cats that have blue eyes when they are fully grown are very likely to be deaf.

Cats' sense of hearing is especially well developed. They hear more acutely than dogs and three times more powerfully as humans. Their ears, in most cases large and upright, can locate the source of noises within seconds, and they perceive even the quietest sounds. Thus they are able to hear mice before they even see them. It is no wonder, then, that a sound that our ears hardly perceive can startle a cat, and that a little bell on their collar is a physical torture for them. Cats share not only the ear tufts and the markings of a lynx, they also have their predatory relative's sense of hearing.

Their whiskers also give them a highly developed sense of touch. The whiskers, located primarily over and under the lips as well as above the eyes, are linked by their roots to a network of nerve endings that can be compared to antennae. They let the cat know that danger threatens or that an opening is narrow or that an obstacle is blocking their path. With the help of these "antennae" a cat can recognise objects and animals, such as a mouse, that it cannot see in the dark. The position of the whiskers also reveals a great deal about a cat's mood (see also the section on cat language).

In terms of smell, dogs are ahead of cats, but cats nevertheless have a much keener sense of smell than humans. There are even a few odours to which they react with a kind of intoxication; you will observe their wrinkled nose and half-opened mouth to maximize the scent, because a second smell organ is located in the cat's gums. Among the odours that inspire such a response are first and foremost catnip and valerian, but also odours that come from people. If a cat is avoiding a person, it could well be because the person's scent is objectionable to the cat. On the other hand, a cat is sometimes drawn to people who absolutely dislike cats, precisely by the person's scent.

Anyone who has ever had anything to do with cats knows very well how finely developed the cat's sense of taste is. Cats can distinguish between bitter, sour and sweet, they have a finely attuned palette, and will definitely reject anything that does not please their gums. This makes it particularly tricky to hide

With their long whiskers or vibrissae, *cats possess a kind of radar system for sensing dangers ahead of time. The position of the whiskers is also a kind of mood barometer.*

The sense of balance in a cat is a phenomenon in itself. During a fall from almost any position, a cat can turn itself so that it lands on the floor on its paws.

129

paws, though there are exceptions that prove the rule. In a fall from two to three metres, a cat can twist itself from almost any position such that its stomach is toward the ground and its legs are stretched out so that the paws land on the ground. The cat's tail acts as a rudder in this situation. This unique method inspired the space agency NASA in their development of a training program for astronauts, who learn to steer themselves by moving their hands and feet as kinds of rudders in zero gravity situations in space.

And last but not least, cats have an inner ear that lets them know when it's time to eat, rest and sleep. They love an orderly regimen to their day's events. It's not just at mealtime that they think punctuality is important. You have to count on your cat waking you up at the usual time every morning, including Sundays, even if you'd prefer to stay in bed a little longer. In the evening, a cat will also wait for you in your bedroom at the time you usually go to bed.

Contented dosing. Those who understand cat language can ascertain whether a kitty is in a good mood, wants to be left alone or feels threatened from the expression of the cat's eyes and the position of its ears.

any kinds of medicine or health supplements into their food. The cat will certainly notice it and ignore the food, even if it is the yummiest of treats.

Another remarkable phenomenon is the cat's renowned sense of balance, which gives felines great acrobatic skill. The cat is able to balance like no other animal, never losing its balance. And when cats fall, they just about always land on their

Alert and awake

Resting

Increasing Agitation

Between Flight and Attack Defensive

Warning

Hissing

The Language of Cats

Even if cats do not speak, people can understand them if they learn cat language. The cat's meow, its face and its body position show us exactly what mood the cat is in, what the cat enjoys and what it cannot tolerate.

When people consider cats devious and unpredictable, it's usually because the

person doesn't understand the cat. Even attacks that appear to be sneaky and insidious rarely come about without a warning. Caution is advised whenever a cat raises its paws, swishes its tail and points its ears back. People who do not recognise or who ignore these signals

should not be surprised if the cat tries to hurt them.

Threatening gestures that nearly everyone is familiar with include hissing and the famous arched feline back coupled with hair standing on end and a bottle-brush tail. Cats in this position, which

When a cat arches its back and hisses and its fur stands out or when a cat rests its head nearly on the ground in a crouched position ready to pounce, caution is always advised.

It looks dangerous, but it's really quite harmless: a yawning cat.

Cats are in the mood for some petting and affection when they bump you with their head and cuddle up, fully relaxed, in your lap. Another gesture of friendliness is the raised tail. This signalises that the cat is in a good mood, is happy and ready to be petted. It can also be an encouragement to follow the cat.

one can observe in particular when cats come into contact with dogs, are arming themselves for defence and for attack. A cat will also arch its back when it awakens from sleep, when it stretches and yawns. This arched back is not at all threatening, but is just a sign that the cat feels comfortable and relaxed.

Cats are naturally cautious. When a cat enters an unfamiliar environment, it will creep around, almost crouching, with its stomach nearly touching the ground. Only when the cat has reassured itself that no

immediate danger lurks will it allow its body to relax.

If a cat approaches you with a tail raised straight up, tiptoeing and purring around your legs and bumps its head at you, that means the cat is happy and has a single wish: to be petted. A cat's head bump is comparable to a kiss, which your kitty will also give you: nose-to-nose, Eskimo style.

The greatest evidence of a cat's love, which is at the same time a demand for affection, is head bumps and "kneading" while the cat is comfortably resting on the lap or stomach of its person. When a cat kneads, it rhythmically moves its front legs with outstretched paws, continually extending and retracting its claws before it really settles down to cuddle. This kneading is the method your cat used as a kitten to stimulate milk flow from its mother's breast, so this movement is sometimes also called "milk-kneading". Cats practice this motion well into adulthood, long after a person tires of it and finds it unpleasant. Truly vehement kneading, although it means that a cat feels comfortable and content, can be genuinely painful for the recipient. The best way to defend oneself is with appropriately thick clothing.

If your cat tiptoes around you with its tail raised straight in the air while meowing, that is generally a signal to follow the cat. They will lead you directly to the source of the problem: an empty food bowl, a closed balcony or terrace door or even a litter tray that in the cat's opinion is insufficiently clean. It may also mean that the cat would like a treat.

You should not disturb your cat if it is lying all rolled up or stretched out with paws tucked in on the windowsill or in an armchair. If a cat is sitting elegantly straight up with its tail wrapped about its legs, the cat would like to be left in peace for a time and will decide for itself whether it wants to cuddle or play any more. You can also tell whether your kitty is feeling friendly, excited or even angry from the position of the whiskers.

These normally stand out to both sides. If the whiskers are flat against the face or angled in front of the cat, the cat is excited, unsettled about something or even ready for attack. Observe the cat's eyes as well: pupils contracted to narrow slits indicate a threatening situation, while large, saucer-round pupils indicate excitement.

Cats are by no means speechless, either: their acoustic repertoire ranges from contented purring to crying, growling and even hissing. In the opinion of animal behaviour researchers, the cat vocabulary includes 16 different sounds that the human ear can distinguish, and these can be sorted into three categories: conversational sounds, calls and sounds of excitement.

Purring and gentle meows are among the conversational sounds that always mean a cat feels fine. Much more variable from breed to breed in their type and in particular in their loudness are the calls that a cat uses to communicate with people. If one listens very closely, the length and pitch of a meow will tell whether the meow is a communication of greeting, disappointment, request to play or feed, irritation, protest or a warning.

Hissing and growling belong to the third category of sounds, the ones a cat generally uses only with other animals. If your cat is sitting on a windowsill or in front of a closed terrace door and clucking like a goose, it has probably spotted a fly or a bird and knows that the prey is unattainable. If you precisely observe and listen to your cat, you will quickly learn its language. You can thus spare yourself misunderstandings that may have painful consequences.

Training:
Like Trying to Herd Cats?

Cats attend the finest of schools: cat mothers teach their children with love, patience and an appropriate level of strictness how to bury their messes, how to clean themselves, how to behave properly in cat play and how to hunt mice. Once in a while there is certainly a little disciplinary tap on the nose or even a swat, but there are also consistent rewards for good behaviour.

As obediently as kittens follow their mothers' rules, they almost always demonstrate a complete lack of understand-

Cats do not want to be disturbed when they settle into this position, which calls to mind the representations of Ancient Egyptian temple cats. The tail is decoratively wrapped around the paws, which are placed close together, and the cat's gaze seems to focus on something far away.

Anyone who wants their kitty to stay off the table and to use only the scratching post to sharpen its claws should summon a good measure of patience. With loving persistence one can achieve much more with cats than with strictness. The earlier you begin showing your cat what you do and don't want it to do the better your chances of success.

Anyone wanting to "train" cats must be very patient, also when it comes to emphasising a "no!" with a quick squirt of water.

It takes a great deal of time to dissuade cats from sharpening their claws on furniture.

ing for any human attempts to train them. There is a reason cats have a reputation for being untrainable, or trainable only with great difficulty. But one shouldn't throw out the baby with the bathwater. While a cat will never fully subordinate itself to a person and like a dog sit or stay on command, with a good dose of patience and love it is possible to dissuade cats from the habits their people find most unpleasant.

You should be very clear about one thing: harshness will not achieve anything with a cat. Loud prohibitions and drastic measures such as hitting will not make a cat obedient, but highly aggressive instead. The only way to reach the cat is to give strict consequences, and this demands a lot of patience. The earlier your attempts at training begin, the better the chances of success.

Even if it's hard to dish out the appropriate consequence to your darling little bundle of wool at times, you must remain steadfast: what was not allowed once is never allowed. Any attempts at

training are otherwise literally about as useful as trying to herd cats. No cat will accept suddenly not being allowed to jump on the table on which it has been allowed to jump for weeks or even months without a word to the contrary, to offer just one example.

It is important that the entire family sticks together, deals with the cat consistently and speaks the same language about setting limits for the cat. It's best to agree on a categorical "No!" which should not, however, be used together with the cat's name. Use its name *only* when you praise your kitten. It doesn't understand the meaning of "No", but it will recognise the intonation and eventually comprehend what you mean.

To use the example of jumping on the table again: Lift the kitten down immediately with a clear "No" and distract the kitten through play. If you're lucky, it will at some point understand that it has no business being on the table. Our cat Crumb understood, but this didn't prevent him from trying it again and again, especially in our absence. As soon as someone came into the room, he would generally leap down voluntarily.

It is more difficult to stop cats from sharpening their claws on upholstery, carpeting and rugs. A deluxe scratching post is no guarantee that your furnishings will remain free of the trace of cat claws. Here, too, simply give the same consequence again and again for the undesired behaviour. As soon as you see the cat scratching where it shouldn't, carry it to the scratching post and guide its paws along the post, praising it a bit.

If a firm "No!" alone doesn't work, a cautious disciplinary tap on the nose, which the cat will recall having received from its mother, is permitted. Or clap your hands, though not too loudly.

Another tact is a light swat with a newspaper, but the common method of squirting the cat with water is frowned upon by many cat enthusiasts as too harsh. Cats are sensitive creatures and quickly mistrust a person if they feel hurt.

Training a kitty to use the litter tray is nearly always completely unproblematic. Place the kitten calmly and resolutely in the litter tray after every single meal, and make burying movements with its two front paws. Follow the same procedure if the kitten decides to do its business somewhere else. After a successful session in the litter tray, the cat naturally deserves praise and cuddling. By no means should you ever force the cat's nose into the puddle or pile of a mishap. Because cats are naturally clean,

If everything is in its usual order, a cat is entirely satisfied. They are easily throw off balance by disruptions.

The more a cat is used to going outside, the less likely it is that the cat will accept being attached to a lead. And even if the cat does accept it, a person on the other end of the line would only interfere with the cat prowling around, climbing and stalking.

they generally understand the purpose of the cat "toilet" very quickly.

Because cats are intelligent and naturally very curious, it is entirely possible to teach them, for example, how to open a door. This can on occasion be very advantageous. Be aware, however, that if a cat learns this, no region of the house will be taboo and that giving a cat this skill does not mean the cat will apply it to room doors alone. Many a cat enthusiast has woken up in the morning to discover that their four-legged friend has plundered the refrigerator.

Attempting to get a cat accustomed to wearing a collar and walking on a lead has much less promise of success. To do this, you must arm yourself with a lot of patience. Begin by occasionally putting a large rubber band around the cat's neck for a few minutes at a time. When the cat doesn't try to tear it off immediately,

you can exchange the rubber band for a leather collar. Keep the cat in sight, however, and always take the collar off as soon as possible. Only allow the cat to wear the collar without supervision when she no longer struggles against having the collar on. Take care that the collar is neither too tight nor too loose, both of which can jeopardise the cat's safety.

Less dangerous is a cat harness that fits around the cat's chest, but even fewer cats will tolerate this piece of equipment. Give your cat the lead as a toy at first, and only then should you make the first attempt to put the cat into the collar or harness. You may even be lucky enough that your cat will someday allow itself to be walked on a lead. The matter of who is taking whom for a walk, though, is entirely open for discussion. Presumably it will be your cat who determines the direction.

Behavioural Problems

The cat is a creature of habit. A cat needs orderliness and a predictable regimen to its day. If something in their behaviour suddenly changes, the cause is nearly always to be found in a change in the cat's environment. If it is possible to determine the cause and to return everything to the way it was, the problem often disappears quickly.

Cats are like seismographs in their awareness of even the smallest changes that for people are tiny and meaningless. This can be a new furniture arrangement or an additional piece of furniture, but it can also be a changed atmosphere in the household. Reactions range from sudden toilet mishaps to apathy and possibly even aggression.

Because changes in behaviour can also have health-related causes, you should consult your veterinarian. If the cat is in good physical health, the you have to systematically investigate the cat's environment and closely examine your own behaviour toward the cat, too. It's often simply a matter of a protest reaction. The cat wants to show you that it feels dissatisfied, neglected or bored because you devote too little time to cuddling and playing with it.

If the situation is something that cannot be changed because you have to be away from home frequently, acquiring another cat as a playmate can be the solution. A cat that was formerly used to wandering about outside will also suffer from boredom if it is suddenly forced to exclusively remain indoors.

A critical situation for the sensitive cat always arises when a member of the family suddenly leaves or joins the household. In this situation, one must offer the cat a good deal of extra attention and love if one wishes to avoid or relieve behavioural disturbances.

If your formerly friendly cat suddenly turns aggressive or obviously avoids your company, you should consider whether you have perhaps deeply wounded the animal, knowingly or unknowingly. In this situation you must gradually regain the cat's trust. This demands a great deal of patience, because hurt feelings sit deep in cats. The most common reaction to changes or conflict is a sudden loss of toilet-training skills. In many cases, this can be traced back to the litter tray itself. Is it new, too small, not clean enough for the cat's liking? Is it in a different place, is it too close to where the cat eats, or have you perhaps simply used a different kind of litter or cleanser when washing it out? If any of these factors applies, it is fairly easy to solve the problem simply by changing things back to the way they were.

Or is your cat now sharing its home with a new four-legged housemate, whether a cat or a dog? In such a situations it often happens that a previously fastidious cat will suddenly use the carpet or a bed instead of the litter box. The cat is defending its territory and expressing protest to you. Sometimes, though, it is simply an expression of fear of the rival. In such a situation, a good measure of extra attention and love are again the best therapy. Once the animals have become used to each other, your cat will begin using its litter tray again.

Because untidiness in a previously tidy cat nearly always has deeper causes, you should under no circumstances scold the cat, but instead quietly and thoroughly clean up the mess. Because a cat is likely to choose to revisit the same place over and over again, it is necessary to neutralise the odour. A vinegar solution is ideal for this purpose since it smells especially unpleasant to the cat's sensitive nose.

Disturbances in cat behaviour that appear suddenly should never be treated lightly. Once in a great while, it might actually be the case that it's nothing serious, but in most cases behavioural problems are a cat's alarm signal. People are generally the triggers for situations in which cats come into conflict with their environment.

> **Information**
> *After decades of behaviour studies, the Viennese veterinarian and animal psychologist Ferdinand Brunner concluded that most cats are perfectly satisfied with their lives and feel distinctly comfortable and content. As he puts it: "One encounters neurotics among them proportionately more rarely than among their owners."*

The Cat Menu

Cats are not Garbage Eaters

A Diversified Cat Menu

Information *If cats don't receive the proper amount of protein, fat, carbohydrates, vitamins and minerals necessary for their well being, they will inevitably have health problems due to nutritional deficiencies. The consequences are not just a shaggy and lacklustre coat, but also digestive problems and serious illnesses that can even lead to death.*

In animal protection legislation that stipulates species-appropriate treatment, proper feeding of cats plays a decisive role. People who feed cats human table scraps are violating these laws and placing the lives of their pets in danger. What tastes good to people makes cats fat and sick.

Aside from the fact that smoked and heavily seasoned foods are poisonous to the feline stomach, the composition of human food does not in any way meet cats' nutritional needs. After all, as hunters of mice and other small creatures they are not so much meat eaters as prey eaters: cats eat their prey whole, including not just the meat but also the largely vegetable contents of the prey's stomach, as well as the intestines containing semi-digested food and the carbohydrates contained in it. Even if we cannot or do not want to serve mice to our cats (even feral or wild cats do not find enough to satisfy their hunger), their food should still correspond largely to the composition of a mouse. This goal cannot be achieved by feeding cats people food.

Cats, in contrast to dogs, are not omnivores but gourmets. This does not mean, however, that everything that kitties enjoy eating is healthy. It is important that their food contain all the nutrients, vitamins and minerals necessary for good health in proper balance.

The ideal cat food is composed of two-thirds meat or fish and one-third grain products. These provide the necessary fibre for digestion. If the cat is fed exclusively meat, illnesses in the bone structure can result, because meat contains too little calcium. Young kittens have an especially high need for calcium, since it is necessary for growth and acquiring bone mass.

The more diversified the cat menu is, the smaller the danger that the cat will show signs of nutritional deficiencies. Factors to consider are their enormously high need for protein—much higher than for humans or dogs. In particular, cats require the amino acid taurine, which occurs only in animal protein. A cat's body cannot produce this amino acid itself and it is thus absolutely necessary that sufficient quantities be present in the cat's food. Taurine deficiency in cats can lead to blindness.

Fats also play an important role in cat nutrition, serving as a source of energy and enabling the cat to absorb the oil-soluble vitamins A, D, E and K. Never give your cat rancid fat, because it destroys the vitamins. Beyond this, cats also require both arachidonic acid, an essential fatty acid that is present only in animal fats, and lineoleic acid, which is necessary for proper metabolism.

The carbohydrates contained in bread, rice, oats and baked goods are not essential for proper nutrition because cats can form the fructose necessary for proper metabolism from other sources in their own bodies. Carbohydrates should therefore be mixed into their food only in small amounts as an additional source of energy.

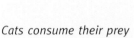

Cats consume their prey whole, skin, fur and all.

The preparation of a cat menu that is properly balanced in every way requires a good deal of experience. For those of us who are not experts, it is generally difficult to determine whether it contains all the necessary minerals, vitamins and trace elements in proper amounts.

Food from a Can

Certainly, the simplest and safest solution is to serve your cat prepared cat food, which is available in a wide range of flavours, so that a diverse menu is also available ready-made. Because prepared food satisfies all the requirements for proper cat nutrition, you need not fear health problems because of nutritional deficiencies. Your animal will be receiving all the nutritional and digestive raw materials that are necessary for its health.

Ready-made food comes in dry cat food and wet cat food. The wet cat food that comes in cans and foil dishes additionally provides most of the fluid a cat needs. Dry cat food is 90 per cent dehydrated, but otherwise is comparable to tinned cat food in composition. This makes dry food fundamentally more concentrated and richer in nutrients. It is very important that cats who eat dry food also take in sufficient fluids. You must observe precisely how much the cat drinks. If you decide that the cat is not thirsty often enough, you should not

serve exclusively dry cat food. Give your cat dry and wet food alternately, or give him dry food only as a snack-like treat. Be frugal in offering your cat the rich dry food, however, if you want to prevent your cat from having to go on a weight-loss diet.

A diversified cat menu is the best guarantee for the health of your velvet-pawed partner. Young kittens require a great deal of calcium.

Even if a cat's food is always served outdoors, it is important to pay consistent attention to having a clean food bowl and punctual feeding times.

Cats are gourmets. This does not mean, however, that everything they like to eat is healthy for them. It is important that their food always be fresh.

Fresh to the Table

If you don't wish to feed your cat exclusively tinned or packaged food, or if you prefer not to use ready-made cat food at all but instead serve the cat food from your own kitchen, the food must always be prepared from fresh ingredients. The essential requirements outlined above must be adhered to in order to maintain your cat's good health.

Even if your finicky feline loves to eat raw meat, it is healthier to cook it. Feeding a cat raw pork and organ meat, in particular, and occasionally beef as well, subjects the cat to a risk that it might be exposed to the virus that causes Aujeszky's disease. This is a sickness similar to rabies, and it is nearly always fatal in cats.

Raw meat can also be a dangerous vehicle for the toxoplasmosis pathogen. If a pregnant woman comes into contact with toxoplasmosis, damage to the foetus can result. For fully grown cats the pathogen does not present a threat, because they simply eliminate it from their systems in their stool. Therefore, pregnant women should leave cleaning of the litter tray to other members of the household.

Poultry must always be cooked before serving it to your cat because of the danger of salmonella, and the same is true of eggs. Never, under any circumstances, give a cat poultry bones. They can result in serious internal injuries.

It is best to be sparing with liver: cats do need the vitamin A it contains, but too much can easily result in a vitamin A poisoning. The consequences can be a stiffening of the joints and deformations of the bones. Raw liver has a laxative effect, but cooked liver constipates.

Serve fish, which contains a good amount of high-quality protein, only after carefully removing all bones. It also must be cooked, since raw freshwater fish in particular contains an enzyme that destroys vitamin B-1 (thiamin), which is essential for cats. Vitamin B-1 deficiency leads to loss of appetite, vomiting and cramps, and it can be fatal. Cereal products and vegetables that have been mixed into meat or fish must also be cooked. Cook vegetables just to the boiling point to maximize retention of the vitamins in them.

Milk or Water?

Anyone who means cats well will set out a saucer not of fresh milk, but of clear water. While milk is rich in calcium, and most cats like the taste, it is unsuitable for cats. It neither quenches their thirst nor sits well in their stomachs. Most grown animals get diarrhoea from the lactose in cow's milk.

The only drink for cats is water, which should be fresh and available to the cat at all times in a clean dish, even if the cat does not drink a great deal of it because it is fed freshly prepared food or with wet cat food from a tin. The moisture in freshly prepared food and tinned cat food covers most of a cat's requirements for fluid intake.

If you feed a cat dry cat food, you must make certain that the cat drinks sufficient quantities of water. A rule of thumb is that for every gram of dry food a cat consumes, it must have three times as much water. Too little water in the cat's system will lead to disruptions in the cat's metabolism.

Actually, milk is not a thirst quencher, but food. If your cat enjoys lapping milk, you may occasionally give it a very small portion of milk that has been substantially watered down. Instead of cow's milk, however, use condensed milk. One exception: if your cat is suffering from constipation, you can serve it undiluted fresh cow's milk as a home remedy.

How much food a cat requires depends on the cat's age, activities, environment and the cat's breed, too. Cats who live exclusively indoors normally require less food than outdoor cats because they use less energy. More slender animals with thinner coats such as the Rex or the hairless Sphynx have a greater need for food energy to balance out their thermal economy, compensating for the insulation from cold provided by a thicker coat (or a coat at all).

Never serve cat food directly from the refrigerator; it should always be at least at room temperature. Cats are even more

Milk is a delicious treat for most cats, but it is often bad for their stomachs. For fully-grown cats in particular, only an occasional small portion of milk should be permitted, and even that should be watered down. Even if a cat who is fed exclusively wet food does not seem to be very thirsty, a bowl of fresh water should always be available to a cat.

How Much Food?

Cats do not devour their food greedily, they take their time eating. They enjoy it and are very choosy. What they ate yesterday with enthusiasm they might well push aside with disgust tomorrow. The danger that they will eat more than is good for their stomach and their figure is significantly smaller than with dogs. Boredom and frustration, however, can turn a cat into a gourmand who will eventually have a weight problem.

Cats do not devour their food with greed, they savour it. Several small meals are healthier than one large one.

Information

If your cat does not eat all of the cat food you serve, remove the leftovers and make the next portion somewhat smaller. Food that is too cold or not fresh can cause diarrhoea. Beside the fact that your kitty will not touch old food, there is a real danger, particularly during the summertime, that bacteria may grow in the leftover food.

The proper amount of food depends on the cat's environment, too. Outdoor cats, who get more exercise than indoor cats, require more food.

pleased if their food is approximately as warm as their body temperature, which is 38.5 °C. The bowl and feeding area, of course, should be absolutely sanitary.

Presumably your kitty will not eat everything you set before it. Even if you prepare the food with great love, now and again the cat simply will dislike what you serve and refuse to eat, no matter how hungry it is. The cat will likely tip-toe around you, offering many nuances of meows until you grant its request for a different serving of food.

Don't forget that your cat expects to be fed on time. Put the cat's food down at the same time every day if at all possible, the best time being just before the

family sits down to dinner. A cat with a full stomach is much less likely to beg at the table. If your cat does this anyway, be resolute in refusing to feed the cat from the table, making no exceptions.

Because young kittens' stomachs are tiny, they require up to six small meals a day, depending on their age and their constitution, after they are weaned from their mother's milk. This is after about six weeks. It is sometimes the case, however, that the milk doesn't satisfy a kitten's need for nourishment as early as three weeks after birth. If the little ones are unsettled after nursing, it is time to begin offering supplemental food.

Kittens have an especially high need for energy, and they also require large amounts of calcium, since they grow very quickly. In their first four weeks they quadruple their weight! The daily energy requirement of a six to eight-week-old kitten is about 630 kilojoules. As they get older their energy requirement diminishes. When a kitten is nine to twelve weeks old, they need only five meals daily. You can reduce the number of feedings very gradually. At about nine months the cat is full grown, and by then it needs only two meals daily, in the morning and in the evening. Long-haired lap cats who don't move around very much sometimes even manage on one daily feeding. But because several small meals are healthier and preferable to

most cats than one large meal, you should spread the proper daily amount of food throughout the day. The average daily energy requirement of a grown cat is between 300 and 350 kilojoules per kilogram of body weight.

Naturally, pregnant and nursing cats have higher energy needs. For a pregnant cat, who requires extra protein in particular, the amount of food should gradually be increased and divided into five meals. A nursing mother cat needs two to three times her normal portion of food, depending on the number of kittens she is feeding.

If your cat is particularly affectionate and loves nothing more than to cuddle up in a warm spot and snooze, you should put her on the scale every now and then. Excess weight is unhealthy for both people and cats, and it shortens life expectancy as well. Therefore, if you determine that your cuddle ball has gained weight, for the sake of the cat's health you should temporarily reduce its daily rations.

If your cat has been able to maintain a body weight within the normal range thus far and you would like to spare yourself and your cat from this routine, which is nerve-wracking at least during the first few days, and possibly longer, try to hold treats to a minimum and keep the cat's weight in mind when offering those daily servings of food. You should never allow your cat to eat sugary food, which is not only fattening but can damage its teeth as well.

Individual cats have quite varied preferences regarding the kinds of yummy treats and rewards they most appreciate receiving. Not all cats love shrimp, sardines, salmon and cream. There are cats who have a great fondness for asparagus tips, peas, carrots or olives. You can be assured that your cat will show you at some point what it loves to eat. We only noticed that our cat Crumb is passionately fond of tinned mushrooms when we saw that the bowl of mushrooms in the middle of a table set for fondue was suddenly half empty!

As long as a cat mother is nursing her kittens, she requires two to three times her normal portion of food to satisfy the whole family.

Cat Care
from Head to Paws

Information

The surface of a cat's tongue is covered with many tiny knobs called papillae, which make it rough like a rasp or sandpaper. It is useful not just for eating, but particularly in caring for its coat. With its long, rough tongue and a bit of saliva, a cat manages to keep itself clean all the time. After eating a cat will clean its paws and then its face and whiskers: it is indeed a true model of cleanliness for every human child.

Cleaning a Cat

Cats have an understanding of cleanliness from earliest kittenhood. Before they can even walk, they clean themselves. As behavioural researchers have discovered, a cat dedicates an average of three hours and forty minutes daily to grooming.

Cleaning is an essential part of every cat's daily ritual from birth until the end of their days. Right after they are born, kittens are licked clean by their mother until they are sparkling clean. Cats require neither soap nor water for the care of their bodies, just their tongues. You may have felt for yourself how coarse a cat tongue is if you have ever been licked by a friendly cat.

With a Comb and a Brush

Even if care of a cat's coat is in principle its own concern, almost every kitty is happy to receive a bit of petting with a comb and a brush. When the cat's coat is undergoing seasonal changes in the spring and autumn you should brush it daily, and otherwise twice weekly. For longhaired cats, daily brushing and combing is an essential duty at all times of the year that cannot be neglected.

While shorthaired house cats manage their coats perfectly well on their own, cats with moderately to very long fur are very much dependent on people for assistance with care of their fur. With the rough tongue, paws and saliva alone longhaired cats cannot manage to keep their long hair from matting, and once long hair has matted, it is not possible to untangle it.

In addition, longhaired cats shed throughout the year, and thus swallow a good deal of hair. The more loose hair you remove through combing and brushing, the less danger there is that the cat will build up indigestible hairballs in its intestines and have difficulty regurgitating them.

Shorthaired cats are subject to the same danger in the spring and autumn, when their coats are changing with the season. This is why one should supply cat grass for them to nibble on: it stimulates the urge to vomit. When your cat is going through seasonal coat changes, it is also a good idea to give it a bit of butter or vegetable oil now and then. Cats like the taste and it helps prevent the build-up of excessive hairballs.

Most cats contentedly lay purring, first on one side and then on the other, and visibly enjoy it when someone combs or brushes their fur. As soon as our Crumb hears the creak of the door of the cupboard in which we keep the comb and brush, he jumps up into the tub, or onto the balcony table in summer, with delighted anticipation. He is the one who decides which part of his body and for how long his coat will be combed.

A cat spends almost four hours a day cleaning itself. With its long, rough tongue and a bit of saliva a cat cleanses itself thoroughly from head to paws.

To care for a shorthaired cat's coat, you need only a fine-toothed metal comb and a brush with harder or softer bristles, depending on the type and condition of the coat. If you stroke gently in the direction the fur grows with your hand after combing and brushing, the last few loose hairs will be removed, too. The coat will be especially glossy if you briefly polish the coat with a chamois, velvet or silk cloth to finish off. Cats with very short or fine hair, such as Rex cats, shouldn't be brushed or combed but just gently rubbed with a damp cloth.

If your cat goes outdoors, look for the presence of insects such as fleas while combing. They especially enjoy nesting in longer fur and can only be detected if one looks very closely. For a longhaired cat you need, in addition to the fine-toothed comb, a broad-toothed comb and a brush with long, firm bristles.

Comb the fur first with the broad-toothed comb and then with the fine-toothed comb. Pay close attention particularly while combing the stomach and between the front and back legs, since these areas mat very easily. It is important that the comb come into contact not just with the overcoat of the fur, but with the undercoat as well. Matted areas that cannot be untangled must be cut out, using only blunt-ended scissors. Finally, carefully brush the entire coat from the neck to the tip of the tail. Occasionally comb and brush your longhaired cat against the direction of hair growth so

that the undercoat gets some "fresh air". The fur will be especially fragrant if you occasionally treat it with talcum powder. Comb against the direction of hair growth, sprinkle some powder on it and then brush it out well. This is best for cats with light-coloured coats, however, because it leaves a grey film on darker coats. By regular combing and brushing you not only do your cat a favour, you also help yourself. Your darling enjoys the additional petting, she won't have as many hairballs in her stomach, and you save yourself the irritation and labour of having to get rid of those annoying cat hairs from clothing, upholstered furniture and carpeting.

Eyes and Ears

The eyes and ears are especially critical places for some cat breeds in particular. A cat owner has the task of checking the cat's ears and eyes regularly to recognise and treat possible illnesses as early as possible.

The eyes of a healthy cat are clear and brilliant. A clouded gaze is nearly always an indication of sickness. You can remove the bits of dirt that occasionally accumulate in cats' eyes in the morning, too, simply by carefully wiping the corners of the eyes with a moist, lint-free cloth. Moisten the cloth with lukewarm water, camomile tea or with a weak boric acid solution.

Good eye care is particularly important for Persian cats, since they often suffer from runny eyes. The cause for this can be the shortened nasal canal or even blocked tear ducts. If your cat has very runny eyes or a possible eye infection, consult your veterinarian immediately.

Cats have difficulty cleaning their ears properly. If there are two cats in a home, they will often clean each other's ears. Even in this case, however, you should occasionally peer into the cat's ears and carefully wipe out the inside of the top part of the ears with a moist and lint-free

Most cats enjoy being brushed because it saves them from having to regurgitate hairs swallowed while cleaning.

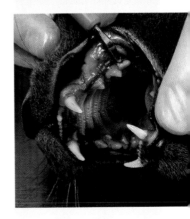

Eye care is crucial for Persian cats, in particular. One should regularly inspect the ears and teeth of all kinds of cats to detect any sickness as early as possible.

Claw sharpening isn't a problem for cats who go outside, where there are many opportunities to scratch.

At every appointment for immunisations, have your veterinarian check and clean your cat's teeth. If your cat seems to prefer mashed and soft food, dental problems could be the cause. Bad odour from the mouth is a distinct indication. Tartar is often the reason, and if it is not removed, the cat may develop gum infections and eventually lose teeth.

If a cat's teeth are in poor condition because the cat has not received enough calcium in its diet, you will have to add calcium supplements to its food. This is only necessary if the composition of freshly prepared cat food does not cover the cat's requirements for calcium. And remember: sweets are poisonous to cats' teeth, too.

Information

Normally you don't need to be concerned about the care of your cat's claws. The cat takes care of this itself, as long it has the opportunity to scratch on trees or a scratching post or board. To the annoyance of their people, cats unfortunately also often use upholstered furniture for this purpose.

Cats take care of their claws themselves. The claws should only be clipped when they are too long, and even then only with special cutters.

cloth. You should never go in too deeply, however, and never use ear swabs for this purpose, because you can easily wound the inner ear with them. If your cat frequently scratches or reaches towards its ears or if dark ear wax is visible, you should have your cat checked by a veterinarian to see whether the cat has ear mites. Ear mites must be treated so that they do not lead to scabies.

Healthy Teeth

The health of a cat's mouth is best served by food that requires the use of the cat's teeth. Cats should be served food that requires them to bite, tear and chew it.

At about six months of age kittens lose their 26 baby teeth. The mouth of a grown cat has 30 teeth. To keep them healthy, you should never cut their meat too small or, if you are feeding them ready-made food, you should at least occasionally give the cat dry food. The harder the food, the better it is for the health of their teeth. If the cat receives too little food that requires chewing, the teeth can loosen within the gums or even fall out.

Claw Care

The sickle-shaped claws of the cat are a multi-purpose instrument: they are useful as a weapon, for holding on while climbing or jumping, or for grasping prey and other food. While walking and sleeping, a cat retracts its claws fully, and when a cat "kneads" the claws are rhythmically extended and retracted. The claws are surrounded by callused skin that wears off with time. While sharpening their claws, cats strip off this skin and thus see to it that their weapons are always sharp. They occasionally assist this process with their teeth.

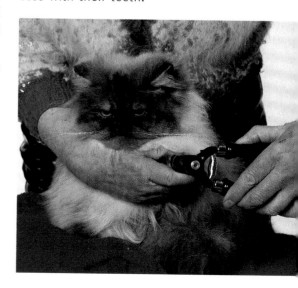

Even if claw-sharpening is a thorn in your side, you should not dull these weapons with scissors. Your kitty will scratch as much as before with clipped claws, if not even more. Furthermore, cats' claws grow as quickly as our fingernails. Cutting is reserved for older cats who cannot sharpen their claws sufficiently themselves, and thus cannot retract them fully while walking.

When it is necessary, crop just the tips of the claws on the front paws with a nail clipper or a special claw-clipping tool. Take the cat on your lap and hold the paw so that the claws are extended. Then very carefully cut only the outermost transparent tips. Caution: there are nerves and blood vessels just past the tip of each claw. If you are not completely comfortable doing this, ask your veterinarian to demonstrate how it is done properly. Amputation of the claws, which is commonly practised in the USA, is a cruel procedure. A cat's claw is more like a toe than a fingernail, and nearly all cat associations strongly disapprove of declawing.

Cats and Water

Cats are by no means as afraid of water as many people seem to believe. Their enthusiasm for water is limited, however. The only genuine lover of water among cats is the Turkish Van, which is known to be an enthusiastic swimmer. Among the rest of the cat population, a cat who voluntarily steps into a tub of water is an exception.

Cats normally prefer experiencing water a drop at a time. While we may be irritated by a dripping tap, cats are very pleased by them. Sitting at the edge of the basin, a cat will swat at it, drop for drop. If you water houseplants, your cat will watch every little stream and even splash in the top surface of a full watering can. If you should ever have to bathe your cat, however, you will need at least four hands to prevent the cat from fleeing.

Fill up a baby bathtub or a large washing basin with only about ten centimetres of lukewarm water (between 30 and 38 °C). Place your cat in the basin or tub so that it can support itself as well as possible with its front paws. Moisten the coat thoroughly, paying careful attention that no water gets into the cat's ears. Carefully shampoo and then completely rinse out the suds so that the fur is not sticky. After drying the cat with a warmed towel, dry the cat's coat thoroughly with a hair dryer, combing it as you dry.

A very fluffy tail on a longhaired cat may need an occasional washing, because of the oil-producing sebaceous glands located at the base of the tail. Clean the area carefully with a mild shampoo and painstakingly rinse out any remaining bits of shampoo. Finally, dry, comb and brush it. If your kitty absolute detests water, you can also use potato flour or a specially prepared, oil-removing powder or lotion for this purpose. Allow it to stay in the fur for a short time, then brush it out.

Information

A healthy cat can go its entire life without experiencing a single bath. So save both yourself and your kitty this procedure unless it is absolutely necessary for the cat's health, which only a veterinarian can judge for certain. The vet will also advise you about which shampoo is best to use.

Cats prefer experiencing water drop by drop. For most cats, a bath is a torture from which one should try to spare them. The only kind cat who genuinely loves water is the Turkish Van cat.

Feline Health

Tip *Inquire about a good veterinarian in your area even before you bring your kitten home. To be certain that the kitten is completely healthy, you should also introduce it to the veterinarian, even if it has already been immunised and neutered or spayed. This is advisable both for kittens from an animal shelter and for purebred cats purchased from a breeder.*

The normal body temperature of a cat lies between 38 and 39 °C. A temperature that is too low or too high can be an indication of sickness.

At the Veterinarian's Office

According to folk wisdom, cats have nine lives and, indeed, cats are exceptionally robust animals. Their coat protects them from many injuries and simultaneously regulates their body temperature. If a cat is fed healthy food and well cared for it need only visit a veterinarian for regular vaccinations. Indoor cats have the best chance of a long, healthy life, meaning that they also offer the greatest prospects of a long partnership.

Even cats who live exclusively indoors, however, are not entirely immune to infectious diseases. Viruses are contagious not only from animal to animal, they can also be brought indoors by people. Prompt and regular immunisation is the sole protection from infectious viral diseases, which often end fatally.

The advantage of an intial visit to the veterinarian is that there is nothing wrong with your kitten, and your new pet can get acquainted with the doctor without being tormented. Place your cat in a transport basket or a plastic cat carrier for the journey. The cat should remain in there for the time in the waiting room as well to minimise the danger of contagion. Always take the animal into the examining room yourself so that you can pose any questions directly to the veterinarian and get information directly from the doctor.

People who know their cats well and observe them closely will quickly recognise initial signs of sickness in their pets that require a visit to the veterinarian. Do not hesitate long to take the cat in to be examined. The vomiting of hair swallowed while cleaning is normal and even essential behaviour, and occasional spitting up of other material is not a cause for great concern, either. If the cat occasionally has diarrhoea and there are no other symptoms, the cause could be food that is too cold or that is not as fresh as it should be.

Diarrhoea that lasts longer than one day and is accompanied by vomiting and loss of appetite is cause for concern. Because cats become dehydrated very quickly, contact the veterinarian immediately if this happens. A cat that is suddenly excessively thirsty also demands attention, since as a rule only sick cats drink too much. In addition to diarrhoea and constipation a dull, shaggy or lacklustre coat, disinterest in cleaning or playing, extremely unsettled behaviour, watery eyes, sensitivity to light and scratching and continuous shaking of the head are all typical signs of health problems.

Cats who are panting, drooling, frequently sneezing, using the litter tray much more than usual or make mournful sounds while urinating should all be brought to the veterinarian as quickly as possible. Anyone who chooses to meddle with the cat's health in such a case and offer it home remedies is playing with the cat's life. Aspirin and other common remedies are poisonous to cats and can be fatal even in tiny quantities. Many

other human medicines are toxic to cats, including all the various cold remedies that contain essential oils. If you have already treated your cat with human medicines, you should share this information with the vet.

If you suspect your cat has worms, mites or fleas, a visit to the veterinarian is called for. You should also take your cat to the doctor if you see signs of poisoning, powerfully watery or even puss-filled eyes, tartar or gum disease. External injuries such as broken bones and wounds from scratches or bites normally heal very quickly in cats, but a wounded animal should still be examined by a veterinarian, since external wounds are often linked to internal injuries that are not visible or easily recognised by a layperson.

For several reasons, you should request a house call from your veterinarian only in the gravest emergency. In the first place, a cat will behave better toward the veterinarian in an office than in its own home. Secondly, the veterinarian's office has a proper examination table, better light, all the necessary instruments and assistants, and thirdly, your cat will forget the pain associated with the treatment much more quickly.

Many vets offer health certificates for their animal patients that also serve as international immunisation records. They contain information about past sicknesses, such as the results of examina-

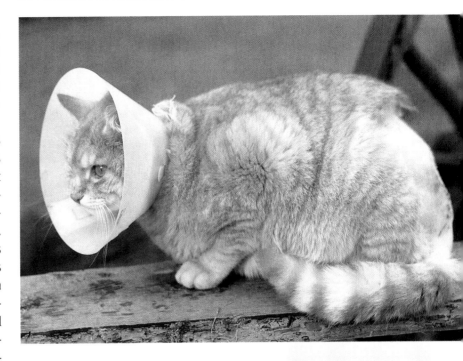

tions and laboratory findings. These papers can be very useful when travelling with the animal, when you move and if you change veterinarians. Take them with you to every visit to the veterinarian's office so that all of the information on it is up to date.

Vaccination offers Protection

While sicknesses caused by bacteria can be treated with antibiotics, most viral illness end in death. The only effective means of protection are vaccinations, and these must be updated regularly, since they offer only temporary protection.

Cats do not like bell collars, but they are necessary to prevent them licking at a wound.

Information *If you have detected any signs of sickness in your cat, you should first measure the cat's temperature. Rub some Vaseline onto a rectal thermometer and gently insert it into the anus. If after three to five minutes the thermometer shows a temperature higher or lower than 38–39 °C, take your cat to the veterinarian as quickly as possible.*

External injuries also merit a visit to the veterinarian, since the specialists know how to examine cats for possible internal injuries as well.

155

immunised against FPV and cat 'flu, and in some cases against cat leukaemia as well. But these are only the basic vaccinations. The vaccination is only truly protective if the cat is also immunised four weeks later. This second vaccination can be combined with the vaccination against rabies. The vaccination against Feline Infectious Peritonitis (FIP) is administered by drops into the nose, but only after the age of 16 weeks. For this vaccination, too, a second dose is required after about four weeks.

The vaccination against cat 'flu, cat leukaemia, FIP and rabies must be updated annually, and the vaccination against Feline Parvovirus must be repeated every two years. Only then is your cat continuously protected from these dangerous viral infections.

Only cats who go outdoors need to be immunised against cat leukaemia and rabies. A few veterinarians are of the opinion that one can forgo rabies vaccination in areas where rabies is not a danger, but that requires that one regularly inquire at the veterinarian's office or with veterinary agencies and immunises one's cat if a case of rabies is reported in the area.

Mites are easily treated at the veterinarian's office, but the treatment should be done as early as possible, because mites can be the beginning of much more serious problems.

The five viral infections against which cats can—and must—be immunised are Feline Parvovirus (FPV), cat 'flu, Feline Leukaemia Virus (FeLV), Feline Infectious Peritonitis (FIP) and rabies. Vaccination offers immunity to the cat, helping the cat build up a specific resistance to the vaccination's target disease.

If your kitten is older than eight weeks and came to you from an animal shelter or a breeder, it will already have been

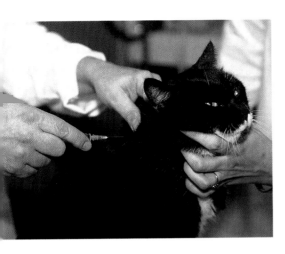

Viral Sicknesses and their Symptoms

Viral sicknesses are often recognised too late, because they generally appear harmless at first. Their typical symptoms appear only gradually, by which time the cat can often no longer be helped. So observe your cat closely and go to the veterinarian's office one time too many rather than one time too few. This is especially true if you have more than one cat, because even apparently healthy animals transmit sicknesses to others.

Feline Parvovirus (FPV) or **Feline Infectious Enteritis (FIE)** is among the most frequent and most dangerous infectious diseases cats can get. FPV is a hardy virus that survives in rooms for months and even years and is generally impervious even to disinfectant. The virus is not only passed from animal to animal, but can also be carried into a home on the shoe soles or clothing. Young cats are particularly endangered. Only a few hours after the first appearance of symptoms, they often pass away, crying pitifully. The first signs of alarm, which are often not recognised as such, are loss of appetite and altogether apathetic behaviour. High fever, vomiting and diarrhoea follow in quick succession, and the diarrhoea is at first watery and then often contains blood. The virus destroys the white blood cells and thus weakens the immune system. Because the virus cannot be fought directly, the cat only has a chance of survival if the sickness is

identified and treated when the symptoms first begin to appear.

Cat 'Flu is not as harmless as the name might imply. It is caused by several different viruses and is generally transmitted by direct contact with other cats. This sickness most often affects young cats, though older animals can suffer from it as well. The first symptom is frequent sneezing. The cat has no appetite and is listless. Initially watery and then puss-filled fluid then begins to flow from the eyes and nose, and the cat develops a fever. Because the mouth and throat are usually also infected, saliva production may increase. In especially adverse cases, the lungs and womb can become infected, and damage to the nervous system can also result. With timely treatment, a cat's chances of surviving this sickness are greater than its chances of surviving FPV.

Feline Leukaemia Virus (FeLV) causes cat leukaemia. This virus belongs to the same family as the AIDS virus that affects humans, but it cannot be transmitted to humans, only to cats. Eighty per cent of the cats who get feline leukaemia die within three years. The disease is transmitted from cat to cat through saliva, urine and feces, and the way the disease exhibits itself varies widely. Symptoms range from apathy, loss of weight, unstoppable diarrhoea and chronic sniffles to anaemia, lung infections, jaundice and cancer-like sicknesses. Tragically,

Regular immunisations are the only effective protection from viral infections. A kitten should receive its first vaccine against Feline Parvovirus and cat 'flu at about eight weeks.

Information

Immunisation is especially important if you plan to travel abroad with your cat. Because regulations about required immunisations can change at short notice, plan ahead and inquire at your travel agency, an automobile club, the appropriate consulate or national veterinary agencies for the latest information. Your cat's immunisations also must be completely up-to-date if you plan to board your cat during a holiday, since the danger of contagion is particularly great in such places.

Cats who are allowed to prowl around outside need the protection of immunisation even more.

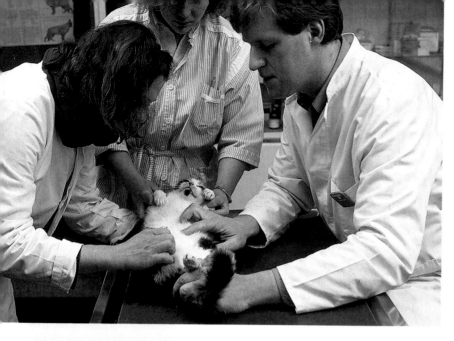

Many viral illnesses begin harmlessly enough and are identified too late.

even cats who show no symptoms may be carriers of the virus and are able to transmit the sickness to other cats.

Feline Infectious Peritonitis (FIP), like feline leukaemia, is always fatal. It is transmitted through direct contact with infected cats or indirectly though food bowls, litter trays, brushes, etc. The first signs of this illness are loss of appetite, weight loss and chronic fever. Later, fluid accumulates in the belly and sometimes in the chest or even heart. FIP can afflict nearly every organ in the body, but the most frequently affected are the liver, spleen and kidneys. In some cases, the eyes or nervous system are damaged.

Rabies is contracted almost exclusively through bites by infected foxes, but martens, bats and other creatures can also be carriers of the rabies virus. The animal who is bitten then becomes a source of contagion. Contact with saliva that contains the virus through scratches or other injuries can also cause the sickness.

Worms and other Parasites

If your cat enjoys stalking about, it's inevitable that it will at some point be infested with undesirable parasites. These not only affect the physical comfort of your kitty, they can also significantly damage your cat's health. The earlier you deal with the parasites, the less havoc

they can wreak on your cat's health. Worms, in particular, are dangerous because they attack inner organs and can impair the immune system.

Tapeworms are usually transmitted by fleas, though they can also enter a cat's system through mice, rats and raw fish. If you notice that your cat is getting thin and has diarrhoea despite a good appetite, you should bring a sample of your cat's faeces to the veterinarian to be examined. You may be able to recognise an infestation of tapeworms yourself if you closely inspect your cat's anus and at its faeces. This problem is usually solved fairly readily by a one-time treatment with a special tapeworm medicine.

Roundworms are particularly dangerous for young cats and puppies who can become infected from their mother's milk. Roundworm eggs, which are usually ingested with the cat's food, hatch in the intestine into larvae that develop into sexually mature worms as they wander through the cat's body. The female worms then lay up to 200,000 eggs per day, and these, in turn, are eliminated through the faeces. If your kitten is losing weight, sneezing, coughing or showing other symptoms of illness, you should first have its faeces examined. Roundworms are also sometimes visible with the naked eye in the faeces or in vomit. Treatment for roundworm infestation is unproblematic with the help of some paste-like preparations. Because these preparations are effective only on the mature worms but not on the larvae, however, the treatment has to be repeated after about two weeks. Many veterinarians recommend that owners regularly examine their cats' faeces.

Fleas are particularly unpleasant little tormentors, since they are difficult to identify and catch, especially in long-haired cats, they are carriers of tapeworm, and they sometimes lead to allergic reactions. Fleas deposit their faeces, which look like small dark dots, in the host cat's fur, and their bites provoke a powerful urge to scratch. Special flea collars offer cats some protection from flea infestation. Aside from the fact that many cats vehemently resist such collars with all four paws, some cats also have allergic reactions to the active ingredient in them. Cats also particularly dislike being treated with anti-flea spray. Other alternatives are flea powder or drops, but be certain if you use these that they are products suitable for cats. Even with these treatments, however, the flea problem is not solved, because fleas live not only on your cat but in your home as well, where they probably lay eggs, out of which hatch a whole new crop of fleas. It is therefore important that all objects that have come into contact with the cat, such as the cat basket or blanket, as well as the floors and carpeting, be thoroughly cleaned. They may require treatment with flea powder or spray, too.

Ticks are among the most feared parasites, because their bite can transmit infectious diseases. If your cat frequents woods or bushes, you should check its skin for ticks regularly. Extract any ticks with a pair of tweezers or twist the tick out with your thumb and forefinger. It is essential that ticks be removed whole, i.e., with the head, or infections are likely to result.

Mites are nearly always transferred from cat to cat, and they can be the beginning of serious sickness. Signs of mites include frequent scratching or reaching toward the ears, head shaking or dark secretion in the ear canal. A strong urge to scratch elsewhere can indicate an infestation of mites in the face and body. If mites are not treated promptly they can lead to scabies, which is also called mange.

Dangers to your Cat

Indoor cats generally live healthier and longer lives than outdoor cats, since they are subject to fewer dangers, but the household itself is not without risks. Especially with young, inquisitive kittens in the home, one cannot be too cautious.

Dangers to cats are by no means limited to an unsecured tipping window or the balcony. Many common houseplants, for example, are poisonous to cats. Even if your kitty has access to fresh cat grass, you can never be certain that it won't occasionally nibble on your houseplants out of curiosity or boredom. The symptoms of poisoning from houseplants tend to particularly affect the digestive system, nervous system and circulation.

Among the plants poisonous to cats are those of the Euphorbia family, including the poinsettia, crown-of-thorns and crotons. The milky fluid in these plants leads to vomiting, diarrhoea, consciousness disturbances and often even death. Fatalities can also result from nibbling on philodendrons, ivy, oleander, Christmas Cherry and mistletoe. Also harmful are diffenbachia, calla lillies, potted azaleas, primroses, narcissus plants or baby's breath. Even chewing on the young shoots of spider plants, which are frequently prized as grass substitutes, can hurt your cat. This plant is not poisonous, but it can lead to a chronically dampened mood.

In this respect outdoor cats are less endangered because they have more opportunity to satisfy their urge for greens. Typical garden plants that can be poisonous to animals include laburnum, plants of the nightshade family such as thorn-apple, hyacinths, lily of the valley, snowdrops, boxwood, autumn crocus,

Frequent scratching around the ears indicates the possibility of a mite infestation.

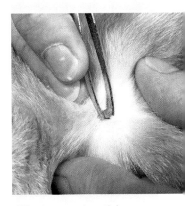

When removing ticks, both the body and the head must be fully extracted.

If you suspect worms, fleas or ear mites, you should consult a veterinarian.

159

Many decorative houseplants are toxic to cats. Plants of the Euphorbia family, such as the poinsettia, contain a sap that can have very destructive consequences.

delphinium, a few types of ferns, potatoes and rhubarb.

Another source of danger to your cat's health that may be lying around in your home are any sharp or pointy objects such as needles, nails, knives and razor blades, as well as many cleaning products and disinfectants. Some substances especially dangerous to cats are phenol, Lysol and hexchlorophenes. To eliminate the risk of poisoning your cat, you should eliminate these chemicals as much as possible from your household. Herbicides and insecticides are also a danger. If you do not want to give up the use of these chemical entirely, you should at least be certain that your cat is nowhere nearby when you use them. Any products containing mercury, coal or tar, as well as acids, alkalis and de-icing compounds should also be stored very

securely in a place inaccessible to your cat. The same is true for paints, lacquers, paint thinner, wood-sealants and poison for snails, mice and rats.

If you have even the slightest suspicion that your cat has been poisoned, take it to the veterinarian's office immediately. Typical symptoms of poisoning include vomiting, diarrhoea, drooling, glassy eyes, cramps, excessive need for sleep and a lower-than-normal body temperature. Prompt injection of an appropriate emetic, irrigation of the stomach and/or injection of substances to counteract the poison can save your cat's life.

Cats only rarely get burned, since they are by nature extremely cautious. If your cat should get burned, though, do not experiment in trying to help your cat, but seek the advice of a veterinarian immediately.

What does happen more frequently is that cats are unintentionally locked away in places, because they have curled up inside a drawer or in a box under the bed or in the back of a closet. More than one cat, too, has found a deathly prison in a washing machine or a clothes dryer. Cats are very inventive in their ability to find places to hide. This is why you should be certain you know precisely where your cat is before you leave the house. One guaranteed way of luring a cat out of its hiding place is to rattle the cat's dry food a bit.

Even fresh grass on the windowsill is no guarantee that your kitty will not also nibble on your houseplants out of curiosity or boredom.

Information *Never try to treat a toxic reaction or an injury to a cat with household medicines intended for people. They could contain aspirin, phenol (also known as carbolic acid) or compounds with essential oils that could be poisonous, even fatal to cats. You should also not attempt to make your cat vomit with a saline solution. Contact your veterinarian to find out what first-aid measures are appropriate to take. Only the veterinarian can judge what is right and necessary in a specific case.*

A Joyful Event

If your female cat is not spayed, you will likely be facing a joyful event before long. This event is only joyful for you and for your cat, however, if you already have reliable people who are interested in adopting the kittens.

Female cats who mature very early may go off in search of mating partners as young as seven months of age. If your cat finds Mr. Right, her belly will begin to swell after about four weeks. She will need extra food and lots of attention and affection. After about 60 days, it will be time: the mother-to-be will become unsettled and look for a suitable spot to deliver her kittens.

If you haven't done so earlier, this is the time to offer your cat a suitably comfortable and secure place for the birth of her kittens, a place that is soft and covered in clean sheets or towels that can be washed. This could be a large basket or a sturdy box opened lengthways. There is no guarantee, however, that your cat will actually bring her kittens into the world in the spot of your choice, or that she will not seek another more hidden place.

Birth usually occurs without complications and without assistance. Whether the presence of people is desired is something the cat will decide for herself. You should respect her wishes in either case, taking your cue from the mother, and either keep your distance or stay near her. Contact the veterinarian promptly if complications are expected.

In relatively short intervals, the cat will give birth to her kittens, bite their umbilical cords, lick them free them from the foetal membranes and eat the placenta. Once all the kittens are born, the mother will wash all of them herself – and then she deserves a reward. Place

Cats that mature early may even seek mating partners at seven months. You won't have to wait long then for the joys of motherhood.

some of her favourite food, along with a dish with a little egg yolk and condensed milk whisked together nearby, and put her litter tray close to her, too, since a new cat mother will not leave her kittens alone. If you then replace the sheets or towels with fresh ones, the mother cat will lay down purring next to her kittens and lick them every now and again. She will be an exemplary mother, offering her children optimal feeding and care.

Kittens, born blind and deaf, being cleaned by their mother. Their sense of smell leads them unerringly to their mother's teats.

Living Together

Cuddling and Playing

Cats are born with a desire to cuddle and play, and these are among your kitty's favourite activities, at least when it's the right time for it. The cat alone, and not any human, will determine when

Not every cat wants to cuddle. The need for petting can vary greatly from cat to cat. When and for how long the cat gets cuddled is not for the person to determine: the animal decides. Anyone who forgets this is likely to receive a painful little swat as a reminder.

it is in the mood to be handled. Anyone who disregards the cat's fundamental desire to decide when it wants companionship, or ignores a cat's warnings to the contrary, will likely receive a painful little note of reminder. So wait until your cat gives you a sign that it wants to play

or cuddle and stop as soon as it lifts its paw in warning.

The need for affection varies from cat to cat. Whether your kitty jumps onto your lap only sporadically, uses every opportunity for intensive cuddling or even demands your attention is dependent not only on its breed. One of the keys to determining a cat's later character is the environment in which it spends the first few weeks of its life.

Kittens who are accustomed to people and receive affection from people from very early on will be much more affectionate throughout their lives than a cat who first experiences affectionate petting from a human hand at ten weeks of age or later, after it has left its mother and siblings.

Something all cats have in common, though is that they will not be seduced into cuddling against their will. Anyone who insists on petting a cat should not be surprised if the cat defends itself and withdraws. If a cat is in the mood for cuddling, it will approach you and might even resent it if a person pets with just one hand and tries to read a book or newspaper with the other. With tentative nose butting or little velvet paws your affectionate cat will request your complete attention. It will also show you

exactly where it likes to be pet the most, and when it has had enough.

Playing, which is by no means limited to kittens, follows the same guidelines. The urge to play decreases somewhat over time, but it remains intact through old age. Playing keeps cats healthy and cheerful and for indoor cats, in particular, it is as important as feeding and other basic care. Researchers have determined that a healthy cat plays an average of 3 hours and 40 minutes daily—by itself, with toys, with other cats and especially happily with people. This is the same time a cat devotes to grooming.

True cat lovers make time to play every day and continuously devise new ways for the cat to avoid boredom. Playing together is especially fun for the cat if you put yourself at the cat's level. Position yourself on the floor during a game of ball or hide-and-seek, or at least crouch down.

Cat-and-mouse is an especially popular game, and one in which your kitty can hone its instinct for hunting. Anything that moves is a suitable object of prey in this game. This could be a toy mouse, a cork or even an empty cigarette box. Tie the toy to the end of a piece of sisal, a long ribbon, an old belt or a stick. This makes the toy easier for you to move and also prevents the cat from accidentally hitting your hand. Your kitten will lie in wait, following the object's every movement, and then abruptly pounce on it.

If you exaggerate the cat-and-mouse game, however, and overtax your cat's patience by keeping the prey out of the cat's reach for too long, the game will no longer be fun. You may then get a reminder that your velvet-pawed kitty is a born hunter who still has sharp claws and teeth. And this experience can be truly painful.

Cats can occupy themselves very well on their own, but they especially enjoy playing with their people. In playing, the cat's innate instinct for hunting makes itself known, even in house tigers who have never really gone in search of prey. Anything that moves can be a suitable object for cat hunting.

Children and Cats

There is hardly a child on earth who has not at some point expressed a desire for a kitten. Both enjoy cuddling and playing, and they have many other things in common, too. It would nevertheless be a mistake to grant this wish too soon. The child must first understand that a cat is not a stuffed animal or a toy, but a living creature. And this is generally not the case until a child reaches school age.

If you have made a decision to add a first cat to your family, try to find a kitten that has already lived with children. This way you will not need to fear that every tiny false move or overly loud greeting will frighten the cat into sticking its claws out. The more you know and can share about the character, personality and body language of cats, the more quickly your child and the cat can become friends.

For young kittens there is a great deal to discover, both in the home and outdoors. The little ones still need a good deal of attention, however, including both a routine of play and lots of petting.

Even with the greatest care, however, you probably won't emerge from this rambunctious game with kittens without any scratches. Keep in mind that a cat's mood can change at any time, without warning, because the cat gets tired or simply doesn't want to play anymore. Young kittens tire especially quickly, because their hearts are much smaller in proportion to their bodies. At the very latest, when a cat raises its paw and pulls in its tail you should end the game.

Explain to your child that a cat cannot be picked up and carried around like a doll or a teddy bear, that a cat should not be disturbed while its eating or sleeping, and that it's not a good idea to run after a cat but they should instead wait for the cat to come of its own will. Show your child how to pet a cat, how to play with it and how the cat sends the message that it would like to be left alone.

If children are too young, they will see the cat as a toy, and they may grab the tail or pull on the cat's whiskers. Even the most well-intentioned and affection-ate petting by a child's awkward hand can be particularly unpleasant for a young kitten. If a kitten has had negative experiences with children, it will never be particularly friendly with children, even as a fully-grown cat.

If things are the other way around and the cat is part of the household before the child, there are rarely any problems after the critical initial phase of adjust-ment is overcome. The cat is likely to at first react with jealousy to the human competition in nappies. This protest reaction can vary greatly among indi-vidual cats. If your kitty is naturally jealous and was up to that point the absolute centre of attention, you should anticipate that the cat may temporarily withdraw in apathy into a corner or even become aggressive. How long this phase lasts depends on both the character of the animal and on your own behaviour. Extra petting, favourite foods and inten-sive playing will quickly convince your cat that it won't have to be without your love in the future.

The cat will then presumably become interested in the little human bundle on

its own and seek its company. In the beginning you should only allow your cat to be near your child, however, while you are close by. You should also keep the door to the child's room closed. If you don't, your cat may well be drawn by the baby's pleasant warmth and odour of milk and crawl into the baby's bed.

The arrival of a baby is absolutely no reason, as far as hygiene is concerned, to give up a cat. Healthy cats that are well cared for are less problematic for small children than contact with stran-gers in the supermarket or on the street.

If cats are used to children, they treat their smaller two-legged playmates more gently than the grown-ups. Even really emphatic hugs from children won't inspire some cats to extend their claws. There is also no danger, hygienically speaking, in skin contact between cats and children.

Cats and children both love to play and cuddle. Once a child has learned how to interact properly with a cat and understands that cats are not toys or stuffed animals but living creatures whose wishes must be respected, cats and children quickly become fast friends.

As long as you have your cat examined regularly by a veterinarian, remove excess cat hairs from carpeting and upholstery frequently and keep the cat's eating area scrupulously clean, there is no need to fear any negative consequences for the health of your children. In fact, the love and friendship of a cat will only benefit the child's psychological development.

Experience has shown that cats allow children to handle them much more than they will tolerate from adult humans. If they defend themselves, it is usually with retracted claws. Your child may, however, once come to experience the sensation of those claws. Then, at the latest, the child will learn that it's best to be considerate and respect the wishes of others.

Dogs and Cats

Dogs and cats speak different languages, but this does not mean that they cannot understand each other. On the contrary, as soon as the first misunderstandings are cleared out of the way, they often become the best of friends. The instinctual hostility that some popular notions imply exist between cats and dogs is greatly exaggerated.

If a dog chases after a cat, barking loudly, it is nearly always the humans who raised the dog to do this who are at fault. If people who like dogs also like cats, then they will find great joy in a friendship between two such different four-legged creatures. It won't take long before the dog and cat understand each other's body language.

In daily life together it will become clear that the same gestures have very different meanings. A dog's growling will at first sound to a cat like purring and a cat's purring will at first sound like growling to a dog. A dog wags its tail when it's happy, and a cat swishes its tail around when it's angry. If a dog raises its paw, it wants to play, while a cat uses this gesture to say that it wants to be left alone.

Especially if a dog and a cat are integrated into a family at the same time, there is no need to fear that there will be anything but harmony between the two.

As a basic rule, it is always easier to integrate a cat into a household that already includes a dog than to integrate a dog into a cat household. The dog will learn to accept the cat as a member of its pack, while a cat, who by nature is more of a loner, learns to tolerate other animals—dogs or cats—in its vicinity only reluctantly.

Allow your animals an initial opportunity to sniff at each other's smells and to listen to each other through a closed door. If you then present your cat a peacefully sleeping dog at first, you have probably already aroused the cat's curiosity. Repeat the contact at a time when the dog has eaten and played hard and is resting in its basket. Once a dog and a cat have become accustomed to each other, they might eventually even sleep together in the dog's basket and drink out of one bowl. They should not share dog food, however, since cats have a significantly higher need for protein.

Travelling with Cats

If it were up to cats, we could eliminate the word holiday from our vocabularies altogether. They are creatures of habit and feel happiest at home. Cats who enjoy travelling are absolute exceptions.

Dogs and cats quickly learn the meaning of the other animal's body language. Cats who have grown up with dogs will not have a fear of large animals.

If you nonetheless want to or must take your cat with you, you should do everything you can to limit the stress travelling can cause cats.

An important place to start is planning for the trip. Above all, you must be certain that the cat will be welcome at your destination. If you are going abroad, find out what immunisations are required by the country or countries you are visiting and make sure your cat has had them. Inquire with veterinary agencies, the consulate, a travel agency or automobile club about current regulations. Immunisation against rabies is particularly important. This has to be done at least four weeks and no more than one year before entry into a country. A few countries demand that immunisations be

A suitcase packed for travel does not rouse joyous anticipation for most cats—it means stress. This makes it all the more important that the cat have a comfortable, familiar travelling container that is also of sufficient size.

notarised or performed only by specially recognised veterinarians.

Even the most peaceful kitten should be transported only in a proper cat carrier designed for travel. For trips on aeroplanes and trains there are specially designed containers with lockable doors. A wicker basket cat carrier with a wire door is appropriate for car travel. Let your kitty get accustomed to the transport container before the trip and feel really comfortable in it. Depending on the temperament and psychological state of your cat, you might consider giving it a sedative. Don't offer your cat anything from your own medicine cabinet, how-

ever: consult your veterinarian. If your cat isn't used to travelling by car or has only gone to the veterinarian's office, take a few short drives with the cat prior to your trip and then have a generous petting session afterwards as a reward. The cat will then not associate car travel exclusively with negative experiences and will behave more peacefully during your journey. Always place the cat carrier on the back seat and make sure your cat is not subject to any draughts, since cats are especially vulnerable to colds.

During car travel in particular, as well as at your holiday destination, it will prove useful if your cat has gotten accustomed to wearing a collar or even a harness and walking on a lead. If you have done this, you will have fewer worries when you stop along the way or near open windows at your destination. Cats who are homesick are unpredictable and may suddenly develop unimaginable amounts of energy in an attempt to return to their beloved home.

It is quite important to take a sufficient supply of the cat's usual food if it is not possible to purchase it where you will be on holiday. Every change in feeding habits means more stress for your cat and can have far-reaching psychological and physical consequences.

Holiday without your Cat

If you don't want to give up going on holiday but do want to spare your kitty the torture of travelling, it is best to leave the cat at home. The cat won't be particularly happy about this and will miss you, but will suffer less than from a gruelling holiday. You should naturally ensure that your cat will have the best possible care while you are away.

Look to your circle of neighbours, relatives and friends for a suitable cat sitter who will offer your darling the care, feeding and affection it is accustomed to while you are on holiday. Children are especially happy to take on this task.

They should not be too young, of course, nor should they be motivated solely by earning money. Make absolutely certain that your cat sitter is both reliable and that they are doing this not out of obligation but because they enjoy it.

You can be very sure you have such a person if you turn to one of the many cat clubs in existence today. Cat enthusiasts join together in these clubs with mutual concern for each other's four-legged feline friends. You can find these clubs through your local cats or animal protection agency, or inquire at a veterinarian's office. If you will be travelling during the high season, you will need to put in your request sufficiently early.

Early planning is also necessary if you would like to board your cat at a private boarding house. If you are interested in doing this, inquire after all the necessary details and don't accept an appointment on the basis of a telephone call alone. Examine the boarding house carefully, because some such businesses are very impersonal and set up only to make a profit. And you certainly do not want to subject your velvet-pawed friend to time in such a place.

Begin looking for an acceptable way to have your cat cared for in plenty of time and never speculate that if nothing works out you can always bring your cat to an animal shelter. Shelters are often hopelessly overpopulated, particularly at holiday time, and hardly manage to care for all the animals that are simply abandoned on the street by their irresponsible owners, even though such abandonment is illegal.

If you will take your cat to a cat sitter or a boarding facility, your cat's immunisations must completely up to date, in the interest of both your own cat and all the other animals there, and you should also give your cat an anti-worming treatment. Your kitty's luggage should include a sleeping basket, a cuddly blan-

Especially well-suited to car travel: a travelling cat basket with a detachable wire door. The cat should be given an opportunity to get used to the container before being transported in it.

ket, a litter tray, toys and the cat's own bowls for food and water, as well as detailed information about the feeding and habits of your cat. Be sure to leave contact information for yourself and your veterinatian with the person caring for your cat. Some places request a trial stay ahead of time, which is a nice idea in

On the way to the animal hotel.

any case. This lets you know how your cat behaves in such a situation, and your cat will know that you will return.

You will also have preparations to make if you have found the ideal solution and your cat can stay at home while you are on holiday. Be sure that your cat and the cat sitter get to know each other before you leave. And so that everything is in its proper order, as is so important to a cat, explain very precisely to your cat sitter what and when your kitty prefers to eat, which toys are the favourites, any other habits and preferences, including how often the litter tray has to be changed. Cat sitters should also know a cat's favourite hiding places, just in case, so that they don't have to search for her frantically every time they enter or leave your house.

Give your cat sitter all of this information and make all of the preparations even if she or he is an experienced cat person. Cats are, after all, individualists and each one has its own preferences and dislikes. If everything goes along as it always has, you can calmly enjoy your holiday. Your kitty might well approach you directly after your return with its tail raised high, but your cat might also initially punish you by ignoring you and only later wind around your legs and purr.

Moving House with a Cat

Moving is certainly no joy for a cat, but it is also not the end of the world. The notion that cats are more place-oriented than people-oriented, which many people used to believe, has long since been proven wrong. Cats suffer much less from a change of residence than they do from a change in their people.

A move is always characterised by lots of chaos and hectic energy, and that is hardly to the taste of peace-loving cats. Try to create an oasis for your cat in which everything remains in its usual order for as long as possible, since even a suitcase packed and ready for travel can throw a cat into a fit of panic or apathy. With proper organisation, a move can be set up so that it is somewhat tolerable to a cat.

Before the stress of moving reaches its climax and the movers drive up, consider whether it might not be worth clearing out one small room entirely and reserving it for the cat. You can place its sleeping basket, toys, litter tray and the food and water bowls in this room and close the door, locking it so that the movers don't unintentionally let the cat out. If you don't have a room to spare, lock the cat along with all of the cat's equipment into the bath.

In your new home, again, initially place the cat by itself in a secure room with all its necessary belongings. Open the door to this room only when all the furniture is positioned and the movers have left the house. Then place both the cat's litter tray and its bowls in a spot as similar as possible to their location in your former home. If your kitty makes a cautious exploration about the place, steps into the litter tray and then eats a bit of its favourite food from its bowl, the worst is already behind you.

Keep doors and windows closed at first, however, just to be safe. Don't allow kitty into the garden for at least two weeks after the move, by which time it should be fully adjusted to its new surroundings and consider the new place its home. Otherwise, the cat might get confused and not find its way back to your new home. And again, you can't exclude the possibility that the cat may feel a great longing for its old home and even attempt to slip off in search of it. If the old home is only a few kilometres away, chances are your cat will even find it. A study by the Zoological Institute of the University of Kiel demonstrated that nearly all cats found their way back home from five kilometres without any significant detours.

With a little extra organisation, a well-loved cat will quickly adjust to its new environment.

Past
and Present

Legends, Folk Tales and Famous Quotations

Cats were not only valued as mouse hunters among the Ancient Egyptians and the Germanic tribes but were also honoured for their beauty. But during the Middle Ages they were reviled as a symbol of evil.

With their enigmatic ways, their strong will to freedom, their grace and beauty, cats have always been a great inspiration to human imagination. Cats figure as good and sometimes as evil beings in legends, figures of speech and quotations throughout the world. They expose the eventful past of the cat, which has been honoured and praised as a symbol of fertility and the love of liberty, as well as for being a mouse hunter, a bringer of good luck and a benificent spirit, but has also been persecuted and condemned as a witch and companion of the devil.

There are numerous legends that tell of the creation of the cat. The Ancient Egyp-

tian fertility goddess Bastet was originally depicted with a lion's head, and many other legends depict a close relationship between lion and cat. According to the Islamic version of the tale, Noah requested a lioness for advice when a plague of mice and rats brought the entire ark into great distress. The queen of the beasts sneezed, and from her sneeze emerged a pair of cats who quickly brought an end to the plague of mice and rats. In another version, the cat is the result of a loving relationship between a monkey and a lioness.

Mohammed and Muessa

There are many different variations of legends surrounding the founder of Islam, the Prophet Mohammed, who was a great cat enthusiast. In order to avoid waking Muessa, the kitten sleeping on his arm, when he was called to prayer, Mohammed is supposed to have cut off the sleeves of his garment without a moment's hesitation. It is even said that a mother cat once gave birth to her kittens in his broad sleeves, and that all cats land on all four paws when falling to the ground because the Prophet always tenderly pet the back of his favourite cat, the said Muessa.

Cats were also honoured by the Germanic tribes. The cart of the lovely ancient Germanic goddess Freya was always pulled by two cats. Anyone who loved and cared for cats could count on protection from this Nordic goddess of love.

There is a connection between cats and femininity in many legends. According to a Hungarian tale, Eve emerged not from Adam's rib, but from the tail of a cat. Just as God was carefully removing Adam's rib, a cat grabbed it and ran away. God grabbed the cat's tail and formed Eve from it. According to a Rumanian saga, on the other hand, woman didn't emerge from the cat, but instead the cat came from a woman. This legendary woman's name, Kata, may well be the source of the English word *cat*.

Just a Silly Superstition

In the realm of superstition cats tend to be portrayed negatively, since most such beliefs originated in the Middle Ages, when cats were considered a symbol of paganism and were hunted down as evil beings, gruesomely tortured and killed. If a cat walks on the altar before a wedding, the marriage will be unhappy. If a cat cleans itself under the window of a sick person, the person will die. If two cats fight in front of a door, there is discord in the house. Drowning or hitting a cat brings seven years' bad luck. When a cat cleans itself, guests are coming. While people in England believe a cat's sneeze foretells rain, in Switzerland there are superstitions claiming that anyone who dislikes cats can count on having a rainy wedding and that anyone who hurts a cat will be showered with hailstones.

The ambivalent relationship between humans and cats is evident in many figures of speech and popular sayings.

Turns of Phrase

Many figures of speech and proverbs that mention cats reveal an ambivalent relationship; some praise the cat's character and others see in the cat an ignoble creature who represents bad luck and deceit:
A house is not a home without a cat. In the cat's eye, all things belong to the cat. Sneaky as a cat. Cats have nine lives. Cats always land on their feet. The cat is biting its tail (a vicious circle). A cat won't leave mice alone (people will do something again and again). To play cat and mouse (to be coy). A fat cat. To let the cat out of the bag (to show one's true intentions). To buy a cat in the sack (to purchase something without checking it first). To set the cat among the pigeons (to pit enemies against each other, or set the stage for an inevitable fight). It's raining cats and dogs (a hard downpour). The cat's pyjamas

(something outstanding). To turn a cat in the pan (to change views or sides for personal advantage). A cat in gloves catches no mice (not getting what you want by being careful and polite). The cat's meow (the best of the best). Like herding cats (futile). She's a cool cat (unflappable). Sitting in a cat bird seat (a favoured or advantageous position). A cat can look at a king (everyone can be curious about important people). Look what the cat dragged in. Curiosity killed the cat. All cats are grey in the dark (appearances are meaningless). Nervous as a cat in a room full of rocking chairs. Like a cat on a hot tin roof. Cat got your tongue? Not enough room to swing a cat. There's more then one way to skin a cat. When the cat's away, the mice will play.

In Praise of Cats

Albert Schweitzer: "*There are two means of refuge from the miseries of life: music and cats.*"

Théophile Gautier: "*It is no small matter to gain the affection of a cat. He is a philosophical animal, tenacious in his own habits, fond of order and neatness, and disinclined to extravagant sentiment. He will be your friend, if he finds you worthy of friendship, but not your slave.*"

Charles Baudelaire: "*Both ardent lovers and austere scholars, when once they come to the years of discretion, love cats, so strong and gentle, the pride of the household, who like them are sensitive to the cold, and sedentary.*"

Rainer Maria Rilke: "*Life and a cat, too: this is an incredible bounty, I swear it!*"

Even if cats are marked individualists, they are also affectionate and loyal.

Cats in Literature, Fairy Tales and Music

Because of their affectionate nature, their beauty and their dignity, cats have always been especially treasured by people who have created works of fine art. Many poets, writers and composers have been inspired by the purring of their four-legged feline housemates and have created masterpieces in their honour.

The fact that the cat was once again deemed suitable for polite company after the horror of the Middle Ages is largely due to the Italian poets Dante Alighieri, Francesco Petrarca and Torquato Tasso, all of whom openly declared their sympathy for this long-reviled animal.

Cats play a major role in many literary works of the past and present.

Jean Cocteau: "*I love my cats because I love my home, and little by little they become its visible soul.*"

Alberto Giacometti, when asked which of his creations he would rescue from a fire: "*It depends on what is in my house. If there were a cat and my works, I would save the cat. A cat's life is more important than art.*"

And finally, a quotation from Colette: "*There are no ordinary cats.*"

In his parody "Gatomaquia", the seventeenth-century Spanish poet Lope de Vega describes a duel between two male cats to win the paw of the lovely Zapaquilda. In the famous fables of Jean de La Fontaine the cat appears as a lover of the gods who has been transformed into flesh and blood. "The Story of Dick Whittington and his Cat" relates an original legend of a poor man who gained wealth through his cat's prowess as a hunter. It was first

printed in 1605 and reappeared in many editions over centuries, taking on a life of its own.

Goethe was another famous cat enthusiast. While the cat Hinze is tricked by the fox in his "Reynard the Fox", in E.T.A. Hoffman's world-renowned "The Life and Opinions of the Tomcat Murr" the main character is a thoroughly intelligent and educated being. William Butler Yeats wrote about the black cat Minnaloushe, staring up at the moon, contemplating and stalking through the grass.

The fairy tale Puss-in-Boots, immortalized in the seventeenth century when Charles Perrault included it in his slender volume of "Mother Goose Tales", lives on and has made its way into modern cinema in the film Shrek 2, with the actor Antonio Banderas lending his voice for the plucky feline. Cats figure largely in many fairy tales, to the delight of children, often playing the main role.

In his "Sonnet to Mrs. Reynold's Cat", John Keats considers the softness of a cat's fur despite its many adventures, and British poet Walter de la Mare described how Jekkel, Jessup and One-Eyed Jill guard Hans' old mill at night in "Five Eyes". How many generations of children have been delighted by the lovely Pussycat romanced by Edward Lear's Owl? In his story "Spiegel the Cat", Swiss poet Gottfried Keller describes how a brave and clever kitten escapes from the evil master wizard of the city, who wants to make her coat into a cap.

Baudelaire's poem "The Cat" and Guy de Maupassant's "On Cats" both praise the four-legged feline housemate in highest

Many famous people were and are great cat enthusiasts who have expressed their affection for their four-legged feline friends in all sorts of ways.

clever detective cat Koko in Lillian Jackson Braun's popular *The Cat Who...* series, and the orphaned kitten Solo and his adventures with a band of feral cats in *Solo's Journey* by Joy Smith Aiken.

Cleveland Amory chronicled the life and times of Polar Bear, a very special cat indeed, in three books including *The Cat who Came for Christmas* and *The Cat and the Curmudgeon*. Another remarkable kitty is introduced in *Thomas Gray: Philosopher Cat* by Philip J. Davis. Thomas Gray continually baffles scholars at Pembroke College of Cambridge University.

Peter Gether writes about his cat Norton in *The Cat Who Went to Paris*, and Rita Mae Brown's grey tabby Mrs Murphy repeatedly proves her unique intelligence in a whole series of detective stories. Mrs Murphy is always a whisker's length ahead of the people in her stories.

The clever cat Francis, the hero of Akif Pirinçci's cat detective novel *Felidae*, achieved fame on the silver screen. Pirinçci became a best-selling author with this novel and also wrote *Cat Sense: Inside the Feline Mind* with the psychologist Rolf Degen. This book discusses what cats feel, think and love, and Francis provides a commentary.

The innate curiosity and proverbial "seventh sense" of the house tiger have moved countless authors to pen cat detectives, some famous, some less so. The number of picture books and children's

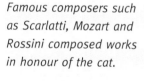

Famous composers such as Scarlatti, Mozart and Rossini composed works in honour of the cat.

terms, as did the French author Colette, who made sure she had constant feline companionship.

The Nobel Prize winning English poet Rudyard Kipling wrote the story "The Cat that Walked by Himself", T. S. Eliot informs us that all cats have three names in his "Old Possum's Book of Cats" and Ernest Hemingway told the story of the "Cat in the Rain".

The cat also figures prominently in many novels and stories by contemporary authors. Doris Lessing describes the rivalry between her two housecats, as well as their relationships to humans and Rufus the Survivor, in *Particularly Cats*. Tad Williams' *Tailchaser's Song* is a pure love letter to all cats. And then there's the

books in which cats play starring roles cannot be overlooked, and the beauty of cats is honoured in a vast array of picture books.

Composers, too, have often been inspired by cats. Scarlatti composed a cat fugue, Mozart a cat canon and Rossini a cat duet. In Tchaikovsky's ballet *Sleeping Beauty* cat music is combined with a cat dance, Puss-in-Boots and the White Cat. Samuel Barber wrote an art song called "The Monk and his Cat", and Alan Hovhaness wrote a sonata based on the pattern of music that emerged from Fred the Cat's paw prints on the piano keys. In a similar vein is Zez Confrey's jazz classic "Kitten on the Keys" and, of course, the Andrew Lloyd Webber musical *Cats* based on T.S. Eliot's poems.

Art and Cats

The cat has never played a more decisive role in art than it did in Ancient Egypt. Even today bronze statuettes as well as images on monuments and grave sites are witnesses to a glorious past of the cat. Only in the Renaissance was the motif of the cat taken up again and portrayed on canvas by renowned painters.

"Genius is required to paint a cat", wrote the French poet and art critic Théophile Gautier, who shared the companionship of 25 cats, including his favourite, Séraphita. Leonardo da Vinci, the great all-around genius, was the creator of the first truly accurate cat picture, though he made it more out of scientific than artistic interest. His "Drawings of Cats" are studies in movement. They show how a cat cleans itself, bends down, creeps, lurks, plays, hunts, arches its back and hisses.

Graphic images of the Fall of Man by Albrecht Dürer include a cat at the feet of the first two humans, and the Dutch painter Pieter Bruegel the Elder drew "The Cat Concert". Cats are also portrayed in countless works by the Italian master Tintoretto, who achieved fame for his wall and ceiling paintings in Venice, in particular.

The picture "The Reading Hour" by Dutch painter Jan Steen shows three children attempting to teach their meowing cat to read, while the French Rococo painter Jean Antoine Watteau painted "The Sick Cat", who is held like a baby and hopelessly resists being examined.

Cats and children were favoured motifs in the eighteenth century. Jean Baptiste Greuze portrayed Eugène de Baculard d'Arnaud, Louis Léopold Boilly painted a portrait of Gabrielle Arnaud as a child, and Théodore Géricault painted a young Louise Vernet.

The French Impressionist Edouard Manet, who painted "Woman with a Cat on her Lap", was an exceptional cat fan. Renoir's paintings "Woman with a Cat" and "Young Girl with a Cat" are both full of romanticism. Even Toulouse-Lautrec, who sought images for his work primarily in the demimonde of Paris, could not resist painting cats. His single cat portrait "Kitten Minette" depicts a cat with a distinctly intelligent expression settled onto red upholstery, a setting otherwise reserved for ladies.

At the beginning of the twentieth century, too, cats remained a favourite motif of many artists. Franz Marc, who loved animals, painted "The White Cat" on a

A statue of a cat with kittens from the Kestner Museum in Hanover, Germany.

"Persian Harlequin in Fairy-Tale Landscape" by Kathia Berger.

yellow cushion, and cats also appear in the works of the painters Raoul Dufy, Paul Klee and Max Beckmann.

The Spanish painter Pablo Picasso had a particularly special relationship with his four-legged feline housemates. He considered cats "the most considerate and attentive of companions", but this didn't mean that he painted them through rose-coloured glasses. He admired their "hybrid" nature, simultaneously gentle and wild. An example of an image of this hypbrid nature is his picture "Cat and Bird". Picasso once said, "I want to create a cat like the real cats I see crossing the streets, not like those you see in houses. They have nothing in common. The cat of the streets has bristling fur. It runs like a fiend, and if it looks at you, you think it is going to jump in your face."

The cat of glazed clay by leading Art Nouveau artist Emile Gallé has its own special charm. One can admire the cat made by the master of delicately-coloured glass with plant décor at the Kestner Museum in Hanover, Germany.

This picture of a "White Cat" on a yellow cushion, painted by Franz Marc in 1912, hangs in the State Gallery at Moritzburg.

The painter Kathia Berger unleashed a kind of cat mania in the 1970s with her artwork. In these pictures Berger portrayed cats in various scenes with oil on canvas, using an intricate technique entirely her own. Her works have became known throughout the world through postcards, calendars and exhibitions. Kathia Berger, who is always surrounded by cats herself, considers cats not just artistic models but creatures of God.

Famous Cat Fans

The names of famous cat enthusiasts throughout history and in the present day are proof that these velvet-pawed and headstrong creatures have been and continue to be prized by many people of artistic bent. Interestingly, among statesmen one finds only a few fans of the freedom-loving cat—and many more who distinctly despise them.

Dictators have always preferred the obedient dog. A bold exception was Napoleon, who made no secret of his love for cats. One of the few friends of the cat among statesmen was the feared French Cardinal Richelieu, chief advisor to King Louis XIII. Richelieu was particularly fond of playful white cats.

Admiral Lord Nelson loved the cat on his ship so much that he neglected his West Indian wife and she divorced him out of jealousy. The French statesman Georges Clemenceau, who was known for his harshness and was also called Tiger, is supposed to have bought a black Persian cat before the start of the Allied Conference in London as a bringer of good fortune. With foresight, he christened her Prudence.

Cats in the White House

Several American presidents can be counted among cat enthusiasts. While Abraham Lincoln was president, his cats were allowed to roam freely about the White House, and Theodore Roosevelt was

completely fascinated by his own cat, Tom Quartz. Roosevelt wrote with enthusiasm to his son "Tom is certainly the cunningest kitten I have ever seen."

President Gerald Ford moved into the White House and brought along his Siamese cat, Cham. George H. W. Bush and Jimmy Carter both had pet cats during their tenures as president, as well, but there has probably never been a cat more at the centre of public attention than the Clinton family cat, Socks. Socks was pictured on the presidential Christmas cards and even received his very own fan mail, which to the irritation of political opponents was answered, all from public funds.

History has shown that few statesmen have been able to warm up to the individuality and marked love of freedom particular to the cat. Almost without exception, dictators have preferred the obedience of the dog.

185

The Cat Door

The English physicist and mathematician

The English physicist and mathematician Isaac Newton enjoyed the company of his cats, but he did not like being disturbed while he was working. And thus, it is said, he invented the practical cat door with an opening for them to slip through so that his kitties could come and go as they pleased.

True Friends

When French writer and philosopher Jean Jacques Rousseau was denounced for his religious views expressed in his novel *Emile*, he fled to Switzerland. He supposedly never recovered from the fact that he had to leave behind his beloved cat, Minette. Theologian, doctor and philosopher Albert Schweitzer, too, known especially for his medical work in the jungle in Lambarene, was very attached to his two cats. They proved to be true friends, waiting patiently outside the operating room until he could accompany them to the hut.

Numerous famous poets and writers have been inspired by the purring of cats.

Purring Inspiration

Poets and writers have always had the most intimate relationships with cats.

Many literary figures surrounded themselves with cats and found inspiration in their company, including Lord Byron and Victor Hugo, Charles Dickens and Charles Baudelaire. Mark Twain liked watching his cat "stretch out on the bare hearthstones", and French writer and critic Paul Léautaud lived in the country with 38 cats.

Hedwig Courths-Maler, the author of over 200 popular novels, is said to have credited her cuddly, purring black cat Felix with his three white velvet paws for giving her the impetus to begin writing. Author Herman Hesse, who won the Nobel Prize for literature in 1946, had a great number of cats. His last companions were Snow White, Zuricher and Winker.

The cat of the French dramaturge, film director and choreographer Jean Cocteau wore a collar with the inscription "Cocteau belongs to me". Cocteau's talent as an artist is evident from his drawings of ordinary street cats. Ernest Hemingway was a proper cat fool. As many as 50 cats at one time lived on his estate Finca Vigia in Cuba, and the descendants of those cats still live on the property. Hemingway's cats had extra toes, and this peculiarity is something the cats descended from them have inherited.

Stars and Kitties

Cats have often been a calming influence on many stars who stand in the spotlight. French actor Jean Marais was a great cat enthusiast, and the German film star O. W. Fischer lives with a whole tribe of domestic tigers. The French singer Georges Brassens, who wrote and composed his own chansons, always had two black cats with him.

Additional international stars who are great cat fans include Peter Ustinov, Placido Domingo, Meryl Streep, Alain Delon and Loriot, as well as international fashion designers Christian Dior, Jil Sander and Wolfgang Joop.

"I often think that many more people should have cats. They would learn a great deal from them about how to get along with people," wrote the German actress, writer and animal-protection advocate Barbara Rütting. She devoted a children's book to one of her own cats, just one of many animals with whom she lives.

For actor Helmut Fischer, who was known as Monaco Franz, the pregnancy and motherhood of his cat Rosy was a significant experience. His advice for what to do when cats do not want to cuddle: "Be kind and wait. They have to believe that they are bonding on their own terms."

Many cat enthusiasts surround themselves with a whole tribe of four-pawed friends at once.

187

Bibliography

Arthus-Bertrand, Yann. *Cats*. Cassell Illustrated, 2000

Bessant, Claire. *What Cats Want*. Metro Books London, 2002

Bessant, Claire and Bradley Viner. *Good Care for Cats*. Smith Gryphon, 1997

Burroughs, William. *The Cat Inside*. Penguin Books, 2002

Carlson, Delbert et al. *Cat Owner's Home Veterinary Handbook*. Howell, 1995

Edney, Andrew. *The RSPCA Complete Cat Care Manual*. Dorling Kindersley, 1992

Edwards, Alan. *The Ultimate Encyclopedia of Cats: Cat Breeds and Cat Care*. Lorenz Books, 2003

Evans, J.M. and Kay White. *The Catlopaedia*. Ringpress Books, 1997

Fogle, Bruce. *Cat Owner's Manual*. Dorling Kindersley, 2003

—— *CATalog*. Dorling Kindersley, 2002

—— *The New Encyclopaedia of the Cat*. Dorling Kindersley, 2001

Haddon, Celia. *One Hundred Ways for a Cat to Train Its Human*. Hodder & Stoughton Ltd, 2001

—— *One Hundred Ways to Make a Cat Happy*. Hodder & Stoughton Ltd, 2000

Hawcroft, Tim. *First Aid for Cats*. Koenemann Verlagsgesellschaft, 1996

Morris, Desmond. *Catwatching: The Essential Guide to Cat Behaviour*. Ebury Press, 2002

Neville, Peter and Claire Bessant. *The Perfect Kitten*. Hamlyn, 2000

Pratchett, Terry. *The Unadulterated Cat*. Orion, 2004

Rice, Dan. *The Complete Book of Cat Breeding*. Barron's Educational Series, 1997

Sands, David. *Caring for Your Pet Kittens and Cats*. Interpet Publishing, 1999

Squares, J.C. *The Big Book of Cats*. Scriptum Editions, 2004

Tabor, Roger K. *Roger Tabor's Cat Behavior: A Complete Guide to Understanding How Your Cat Works*. Betterway Books, 1998

Taylor, David. *Think Cat: An Owner's Guide to Feline Psychology*. Cassell Illustrated, 2004

Thomas, Heather. *Care for Your Kitten (RSPCA Pet Guides)*. Collins, 2004

Acknowledgements
We would like to thank all the cat enthusiasts and cat associations that have supported us with their expert advice. We would like to extend special thanks to the German Cat Enthusiasts Club (Verein Deutscher Katzenfreunde) and to the veterinarian Dr. Clemens Niemann.

Addresses

Animal Protection Associations

Animal Protection Trust
Coldlands Farm
Haroldslea
Horley
Surrey RH6 9PJ
Tel: +44 (0)01737 221280
(Lost & Found Register)
Tel: +44 (0)1403 732500)
http://www.animalprotectiontrust.
org.uk

Royal Society for the Prevention
of Cruelty to Animals (RSPCA)
Wilberforce Way
Southwater
Horsham
West Sussex RH13 9RS
Tel: +44 (0)870 3335 999
http://www.rspca.org.uk

National Animal Welfare Trust
Headquarters, London and
home counties animal rescue centre
Tyler's Way
Watford-By-Pass
Watford
Hertfordshire WD25 8 WT
Tel: +44 (0)20 8950 0177
http://www.nawt.org.uk

Cat Associations

Cats Protection
National Cat Centre
Chelwood Gate
Haywards Heath
Sussex RH17 7TT
Tel: +44 (0)8702 099 099
http://www.cats.org.uk

Feline Advisory Bureau
'Taeselbury'
High Street
Tisbury
Wiltshire
SP3 6LD
Tel: +44 (0)870 742 2278
http://www.fabcats.org

Breed Cat Associations

Fédération Internationale Féline
(F.I.Fe)
General Secretary
Mrs Penelope Bydlinski
Little Dene, Lenham Heath
Maidstone
Kent ME17 2BS
Tel: +44 (0)1622 850913
http://www.fifeweb.org/

The Governing Council of
the Cat Fancy (GCCF)
4—6 Penel Orlieu
Bridgwater, Somerset
TA6 3PG
Tel: +44 (0)1278 427575
http://ourworld.compuserve.com/hom
epages/GCCF_CATS/index.htm

World Cat Federation (WCF)
Geisbergstr. 2
D-45139 Essen
Germany
Tel.: +49 (0)201 555724
http://www.wcf-
online.de/english/index.htm

National Clubs and Organisations

National Cat Club
http://www.nationalcatclub.co.uk/

Felis Britannica
http://www.felisbritannica.co.uk/
index.htm

Everycat UK
http://www.everycat-uk.co.uk/

Scottish Breeds Association
http://www.sbacats.co.uk

Siamese and All Breeds Cat Club
of Ireland
http://www.sabcci.com

Note: There are countless local,
regional, national and international
clubs and organisations devoted to
cats in some way. Area clubs cater
for all kinds of cats, including
ordinary house cats, while breed
clubs focus on a specific type of cat.
The groups listed above are just a
few of the rich resources available
to you.

Index

Archiv für Kunst und Geschichte,
Berlin p. 184 (b.)

Editorial team "Ein Herz für Tiere":

Cogis/Amblin p. 6, 32 (t.), 172

Cogis/DR p. 170

Cogis/Garguil p. 169 (t.)

Cogis/Gengoux p. 89

Cogis/Gissey p. 40/41

Cogis/Labat, J. c. p. 44 (b. r.), 46,
47, 48 (t. l. and b. l.), 49 (t.), 54 (b.),
60 (t. and b.), 67, 68, 69 (r.), 71,
73, 74 (t.), 76 (b.), 77, 81, 84 (b.),
85 (r.), 88 (t.), 90, 92, 94, 96 (b.),
100 (t. l. and b. l.), 128 (t. r.), 133 (t.),
148 (t.), 150 (b.), 151, 168 (b. r.),
185 (t.), 186 (t.)

Cogis/Lanceau, Yves p. 43 (t. l. and
t. r.), 50 (t. and b.), 51, 52, 53 (t.),
56, 57 (b.), 62, 63 (t.), 69 (l.), 74 (b.),
76 (t. l.), 82, 83 (b.), 91 (b.), 95 (b.),
97, 98, 99 (c. r.), 104/105, 106 (b.),
108 (t.), 131 (b.), 167 (b.), 177

Cogis/Labat/Lanceau p. 79, 80
(t. and c.), 86, 129 (b.), 131
(t. r.), 149 (b. r.), 187 (b.)

Cogis/Lili p. 128 (b. r.)

Cogis/Vidal p. 45 (t.), 129 (t.), 186 (b.)

Cogis/WARA p. 157 (t.)

Berger, Kathia p. 184 (t.)

Frechen, Monika p. 64 (c.)
Heinz, Heide p. 123 (c. r.)

Kestner-Museum, Hannover p. 12,
13 (l.), 183

Neckermann p. 119 (b. l.)

Okapia KG Bildarchiv, Frankfurt/Berlin
p. 10 (b.), 131 (t. l.)

Reinhard-Tierfoto, Heiligkreuzsteinach
p. 10 (t.), 11, 16 (t. l., b. l. and b. r.),
17 (b.), 19 (b.), 20 (t. and b.), 23, 26 (t.),
27, 28, 29, 30 (t.), 31 (b.), 32 (b.), 33
(t. and b.), 34 (t.), 35, 36 (t.), 37 (t.),
38, 39, 48 (t. r. and b. r.), 49 (b.),
53 (b.), 55, 57 (t.), 59 (b. r.), 63 (b. l.
and b. r.), 64 (t.), 65, 66 (t. l. and t. r.),
72 (t.), 72 (b. r.), 75, 76 (t. r.), 78,
80 (b.), 83 (t.), 85 (t. l. and b. l.), 87
(t. and b.), 91 (t.), 95 (t. l. and t. r.),
99 (b. l.), 100 (b. r.), 103 (t. and b.),
107 (b.), 108 (b.), 110 (b.), 111, 112 (t.),
114 (t. l.), 115 (t. r. and b. r.), 118, 119
(b. r.), 120 (t. and b.), 121, 122, 123
(c. l. and b. r.), 126 (t. and b.), 132 (b.),
134 (b.), 135, 138/139, 140, 141 (t. and
b.), 142 (b.), 143 (t. and b.), 145, 148
(b.), 149 (t. r.), 154, 155 (t.), 156 (b.),

157 (b.), 158,159 (t. r. and b. r.), 160
(t. and b.), 161 (t. c. and b.), 165,
169 (b.), 176, 178, 179, 180 (t.), 181

Schanz, Ulrike p. 21 (b.), 26 (b.), 58,
60 (c.), 61, 70, 99 (b. r.), 101, 112 (b.),
113 (b.), 114 (t. r.), 117 (t.), 133 (b.),
144 (t.), 149 (t. r. and b. l.), 164 (b.),
166 (r.), 173

Silvestris, Kastl p. 8/9, 13 (t.), 14 (b.),
15 (t.), 17 (t.), 18 (t. and b.), 19 (t.),
21 (t.), 24/25, 30 (b.), 31 (t.), 36 (b.),
37 (b.), 42, 43 (b.), 44 (l. and t. r.),
45 (b.), 47 (c.), 54 (t.), 64 (b.), 66
(b.), 72 (b. l.), 84 (t.), 88 (b.), 93,
96 (t.), 99 (t.), 106 (t.), 109, 110 (t.),
112 (t.), 115 (t. l. and b. l.), 116,
119 (t. l. and t. r.), 123 (t.), 124/125,
127, 128 (c. b.), 130 (t.), 132 (t.),
134 (t.), 136, 140 (l.), 141 (c.), 142 (t.),
144 (b.), 146/147, 150 (t.), 152/153,
155 (b.), 156 (t.), 159 (l.), 166 (l.),
167 (t.)168 (t. and b. l.), 174/175,
180 (b.), 182 (t. and b.), 187 (t.)

Skogstad, Karin p. 59 (t. and b. l.),
117 (b.), 128 (c. r.), 162/163, 185 (b.)

Verein Dt. Katzenfreunde e.V.,
Hamburg, Germany
p. 14 (t.), 15 (b.), 22 (t. and b.),
34, 107 (t.), 114 (b.),127 (b.),
130 (b.), 164 (t.)

t. = top, b. = bottom, c. = center